FERRY & CRUISE

annual
2011

Published by:
Ferry Publications, PO Box 33, Ramsey, Isle of Man IM99 4LP
Tel: +44 (0) 1624 898446 Fax: +44 (0) 1624 898449
E-mail: ferrypubs@manx.net Website: www.ferrypubs.co.uk

CONTENTS

INTRODUCTION

The third edition of Ferry Publications' 'Ferry & Cruise Annual' very much continues along the same lines that have proved to be so popular with our readership in recent years.

With the global economic recession, times have been difficult for the ferry and cruise industries and there has been an inevitable loss of ships and operators. In this edition we cover the history of the *Mona Lisa*, which finished her career in 2010 and as Swedish America's *Kungsholm* was the last Clyde-built passenger liner. The implementation of SOLAS 2010 has sadly seen the demise of a number of notable cruise vessels although the arrival of new vessels has continued even though order books have thinned. The Italian Fincantieri yards continue to produce a glittering array of modern cruise ships which are the subject of an in-depth examination. Some operators continue to concentrate on the traditional aspects of cruising and offer a solidly British-style experience. Fred. Olsen Cruise Lines is one such operator and a Baltic cruise on board their flagship Balmoral is described.

The ferry industry has suffered from a great deal of over-capacity and fleet and route contraction has been an inevitable consequence. However, with the restart of the Cork route, it appears that a niche market continues to flourish and this is celebrated in our article on the Cork Connection. Elsewhere the busy and flourishing network of routes and ferries to Morocco is given special treatment while, as they are dispersed across the globe, the iconic 'Superfast' series of conventional high-speed ships is discussed and assessed.

Our commitment to high-quality photographs and photographic reproduction is assured and we also present features concerning the passenger shipping at Guernsey, across the Irish Sea and in the ports of Piraeus and Istanbul.

Miles Cowsill & John Hendy
October 2010

*Sealink's former **Galloway Princess** is seen arriving at Algeciras in September 2010 with Gibraltar in the background. Today she sails as the **Le Rif**. (Bruce Peter)*

1 A Baltic Cruise in Fred. Olsen's *Balmoral*

by John Hendy

The Fred. Olsen Cruise Lines motor vessel *Balmoral* was built at Jos. L. Meyer's Papenburg yard in Germany as the *Crown Odyssey*. She was launched in November 1987 for service with the Greek-owned, American-financed Royal Cruise Line of Piraeus and many of her internal glass doors retain their original crown motif to this day.

As built, the ship measured 217.9 metres with a 28.2-metre beam and a 6.8-metre draught. Her lines were fairly typical of that period and she boasted a handsome, if rather exaggerated, bow, compact lines and a transom stern. At 34,242 gross tons the ship was capable of cruising at speeds of up to 22.5 knots, her four MAK diesels developing 21,300 kW. Passenger accommodation was usually for 1,104 although a maximum of 1,230 could be carried.

The *Crown Odyssey* was delivered during June 1988 and operated her first cruise between Emden and Tilbury. Two years later the ship was reflagged in the Bahamas and in 1992 she was sold to Kloster Cruises. In May 1995 she became the *Norwegian Crown* for their Norwegian Cruise Line but five years later reverted to *Crown Odyssey* for service with subsidiary company Orient Line. With this completed, the vessel was again renamed *Norwegian Crown* whilst undergoing refit in Singapore. The extremely unattractive fitness centre was added above the bridge at this period.

Looking to expand their fleet, Fred. Olsen Cruise Lines (FOCL) purchased the vessel in 2006 for delivery in the following November and she duly arrived for major surgery at Blohm & Voss at Hamburg on 15th November 2007. There she was cut in two and a 30-metre section with 186 new passenger cabins was inserted. This had been built by Schichau Seebeckwerft at Bremerhaven and towed to Hamburg at the end of October. In keeping with the Olsen nomenclature, the stretched ship was named *Balmoral*; gross tonnage was raised to 43,537 and passenger numbers to

1,400. The *Balmoral* duly arrived at Dover on 25th January 2008 to carry out her maiden voyage but the work was not completed and her first cruise with FOCL was therefore cancelled until 13th February when she sailed to the West Indies.

PROLOGUE

With such an iconic name as *Balmoral*, even before stepping on board her passengers would surely have made associations with traditional furnishings combined with the comforts of a capacious Scottish country mansion in the best baronial style of the landed gentry. The ship is unashamedly British in character. Her fittings are restrained and easy on the eye, she is both quiet in nature and quiet in character with much use having been made of browns and greens to create a restful and peaceful environment in which to enjoy a cruise. Her subdued interior is quite unlike the more recently built floating cruise resorts of the 'bling' generation with futuristic interiors, bright lights and music pounding on every deck and in every bar. It is therefore hardly surprising that the general perception of FOCL vessels is that they are directed at attracting the older end of the market which was very much the overall impression that my wife and I gained when we boarded the ship at Dover in June for a 12-night Baltic cruise.

ON BOARD

Passenger accommodation in the *Balmoral* stretches between Decks 3 and 11 with crew cabins down below the water line on Deck 2. The ship's eating areas are clustered at her after end with the principal Ballindalloch Restaurant being sited on Deck 6. With the increase of passengers following the ship's stretching, extra restaurants were created on Deck 10 with the mirror-imaged smaller Avon Restaurant (starboard side) and Spey Restaurant (port

This remarkable picture shows the ship's new 30-metre section ready for insertion at Blohm & Voss during late 2007. The Spey Restaurant is being constructed on the funnel's port side. (Blohm & Voss, Hamburg)

On board the **Balmoral** leaving Dover for the Baltic (via the Kiel Canal) on the afternoon of 20th June. At the forward end, Deck 11 houses the ship's Observation Lounge and Marquee Bar. (John Hendy)

The ship's spacious and comfortable library is situated on the port side of the new section of Deck 7. (John Hendy)

*The **Balmoral** is seen approaching the South Foreland. (FotoFlite)*

Fred. Olsen Cruise Lines

side). We were seated in the latter and a more splendid position would have been difficult to find giving excellent panoramic views of the passing seascapes. One drawback with the *Balmoral* is her lack of outside deck space and these two fine restaurants unfortunately swallowed up a large area which had previously been allocated to passenger relaxation. For those passengers preferring a less formal setting, the Palms Café on Deck 7 proved to be a large and popular area at lunch and tea times. On the deck above aft, were the Lido Lounge and bar which spilled out onto the open deck overlooking one of the ship's two swimming pools. The Lido Bar is housed within a large 'glass house' of recent construction.

The main entertainment area is the Neptune Lounge forward on Deck 7. This comfortable area of tiered seating is the centre for the evening shows, lectures and other performances as well as the morning meeting place for shore excursions. Since the ship was stretched, it is probably now too small and evening shows are split into two sittings to coincide with meal times.

Between the Palms Café (aft) and the forward Neptune Lounge, Deck 7 also contains the Morning Light Pub and in the newly inserted section, the ship's spacious library, adjacent card room and internet room (all port side) and the Braemar Lounge (starboard side). Forward of this is the main reception area and atrium which links Deck 6 with Deck 7. Here are sited the ship's offices and shops and during the evenings, tables were laid out selling a variety of (very indifferent) Russian souvenirs.

The bridge is situated on Deck 9 and above this are the beauty salon and fitness centre. Although added before Olsen took over the ship, this space is undoubtedly wasted with the best views on board reserved for a very small minority of people not interested in the views. Surely it would make more sense to move both salon and fitness centre to Deck 3 and create a superb observation lounge in the space they vacate.

The top deck is Deck 11 on which passengers may walk around the funnel, relax on sunbeds behind glass screens or make use of the ship's second pool. Forward is the Observatory Lounge and Marquee Bar in which nightclub-style piano music was played during the evenings and which proved to be a very relaxing after dinner area to sit and chat.

For those passengers who might enjoy uninterrupted views of the sea, the after end of Deck 11 proved ideal but was the only place on board from where one could gain a clear view forward. Deck 7 provided a pleasant promenade around the bridge front and below the lifeboats and four complete circuits of this deck equated to one mile.

BALTIC BEAUTY

Our Baltic Beauty cruise lasted 12 nights and included four complete days at sea which I personally enjoyed. Leaving the new *Seabourn Sojourn* astern at Dover's Admiralty Pier, the *Balmoral* headed through the western exit of Dover Harbour at 16.30 on 20th June on her 415 nautical mile leg to Kiel.

Approaching an almost featureless German coast, we took on the Elbe pilot from the Swath vessel *Borkum* at 15.05 the following day and passed Cuxhaven some 90 minutes later. The ro-ro vessels *Ark Forwarder* and *Tor Futura* were alongside and once in the river, we finally arrived at Brunsbuttel at 18.00. After a fascinating overnight transit of the Kiel Canal, passing on our way firstly Phoenix Reisen's *Albatros* followed 90 minutes later in the gloom by their exceptionally rowdy *Amadeus,* our first port of call the following morning was Kiel where the ship berthed at the Ostseekai.

A casual stroll along the quayside during the port's regatta week revealed a variety of craft ancient and modern and included sail, steam and diesel-propelled vessels. Stena Line's *Stena Scandinavica* was berthed astern of us while the *Color Magic* was moored on the far side of the harbour. During

dinner, we were able to watch the 'Scandinavica' depart for Gothenburg before sailing ourselves into a mirror-like Baltic.

Following a further day at sea passing a procession of distant ro-ro vessels from the Transfennica, Stena, Tallink, Scandlines and Finnlines fleets we arrived at Tallinn, capital of Estonia and moored at the new cruise port adjacent to Royal Caribbean's *Vision of the Seas*. With the present size of the Tallink fleet, there was always the chance of seeing ferries and sure enough, the *Superstar*, *Baltic Queen* and *Baltic Prince* were in port before the former left for Helsinki while Eckero's *Nordlandia* (ex *Olau Hollandia*) arrived from the Finnish capital shortly after us. The rather forlorn sight of the *Vana Tallinn* (ex *Dana Regina*) tucked away in a dockyard to the west reminded me of happier days on the Esbjerg service.

Viking Line's *Viking XPRS* was in port during the later afternoon and the *Nordlandia* followed us out as we departed for the 190 nautical mile sailing to St Petersburg.

The new cruise terminal at the Russian port has been built on reclaimed land to the west of the city and from the decks of the *Balmoral*, little was visible on the landward side apart from piles of sand backed by rows of faceless, grey apartment blocks; welcome to the former Soviet Union.

Berthed at right angles to the *Balmoral* was the P&O Princess Cruises' *Star Princess,* doing a passable impersonation of a floating supermarket trolley, and we were soon joined by the *Vision of the Seas*. The smaller cruise ships continue to berth in the River Neva and during the next 24 hours, the *Silver Whisper, Silver Cloud* and the new *Seabourn Sojourn* all moored there. Six cruise ships in port inevitably made our visits to the palaces and museums rather crowded and a degree of enjoyment was inevitably lost in the scrum.

St Petersburg seems to have its own system of weather and during our stay there we received our only rain of the cruise. We also witnessed the arrival of a British-built ship, the Madeira-registered *Princess Danae* (ex *Port Melbourne*) which berthed ahead of us although just how much longer this venerable vessel and her sister will continue (or be allowed to continue) remains to be seen.

Knowing that I was on board, FOCL had kindly arranged for me to meet Captain Atle Knutsen on the ship's bridge. Bergen-based Captain Knutsen had only recently been transferred to the *Balmoral* from the *Boudicca* and was enjoying the challenge of getting to know his new ship. The first vessel in which he had served was the *Albatros* and so he was very familiar with the *Royal Viking Star* trio of cruise ships and holds them in very high regard. The *Balmoral*'s bridge layout, including her open bridge wings, was certainly in keeping with the rest of the ship.

At Helsinki we were the only cruise ship in port and we berthed at right angles to the Viking Line terminal adjacent to where the *Mariella* later docked. The *Silja Serenade* also arrived later that morning. After the rather claustrophobic atmosphere of St Petersburg, the Finnish capital proved to be a breath of fresh air.

The overnight crossing to Stockholm was another 246 nautical miles and the *Balmoral* berthed at Frihamnen adjacent to the Silja Line terminal in the east of the city. The *Silja Serenade* followed us in from Helsinki, the *Silja Festival* arrived from Riga and the *Victoria I* came in from Tallinn while the *Silja Europa* left for Turku.

A short bus trip into the city revealed the *Jewel of the Seas* berthed downstream from the Viking Line terminal and the arrival of the ancient but splendid *Birger Jarl*, the *Viking Cinderella* and then the *Birka Princess* from Aland. The harbour is always bustling with a variety of passenger craft, many of considerable vintage and all providing much interest. Before the *Balmoral* departed on the 441 nautical mile sailing to Copenhagen, the *Galaxy* arrived

The main foyer area as seen from Deck 7 looking aft into the new section. On the deck below are the ship's Reception (right) and Shore Tours Office desks (left) while the corridor (centre, below the model) leads through to the Ballindalloch Restaurant. (John Hendy)

The Ballindalloch Restaurant on Deck 6 is the ship's main dining area although the Spey and Avon Restaurants (on Deck 10) were subsequently added during her stretching. (John Hendy)

*Passing Phoenix Reisen's **Albatros** in the Kiel Canal, Captain Knutsen is taking photographs of his old ship! (John Hendy)*

*The **Balmoral** alongside the Ostseekai at Kiel during the port's annual regatta week. (John Hendy)*

*At Tallinn, the **Balmoral** was joined by Royal Caribbean's **Vision of the Seas** which represented a totally different style of cruising experience. (John Hendy)*

*Welcome to Russia! Looking across the **Balmoral**'s spotless fo'c'sle towards the ancient Portugese-registered **Princess Danae** (ex **Port Melbourne** of 1955). The new cruise port at St Petersburg is built on reclaimed land to the west of the city. (John Hendy)*

from Turku replacing the *Victoria I* at the berth. A particular highlight was passing the *Amorella* shortly after joining the main channel out of Stockholm.

The three and a half hour sail through the Stockholm archipelago is always enjoyable but all too soon the following *Viking Cinderella* changed course for Aland and the *Balmoral* headed out on a more southerly track. These were new waters for me as the *Balmoral* wove in and out of the pattern of islands and onwards towards the open sea.

With the ship running on her starboard engine at 13 knots, we made a leisurely overnight passage passing between Gotland and Oland. By 15.00 the following day we were off the Swedish port of Karlskrona and shortly afterwards passed the freighter *Stena Forerunner* on charter to Transfennica. For most of the afternoon I had been watching a vessel which slowly gained on us as the day wore on. By the early evening she was in our wake before suddenly turning and running down our port side with the full sun on her. This proved to be Scandline's ro-pax vessel *Urd* which I had known at Dover in the 1980s as Sealink's *Seafreight Highway* and which was on her way to Travemunde from Ventspils.

The *Balmoral* arrived at Copenhagen's Langeliniekaj at 06.45 the following morning with Polferries' *Pomerania* following us in. Instead of berthing in the heart of the city, the ferries now berth at the northern end of the dock system and DFDS' *Pearl of Scandinavia* (from Oslo) also entered port during breakfast. NCL's *Norwegian Sun* was nearby as was one of the twin Azamara ships while a little further down towards the city centre lay the *Silver Whisper*.

With all passengers on board by 13.30, we were scheduled for departure at 14.00 but engine problems delayed matters. There was apparently not enough air in the system to fire up one of the engines and so it required bleeding which meant a four-hour delay. We learned from the Captain the following day, that the problem had been more serious than at first anticipated and that it was not until 23.30 that the engine was up and running properly. Even then, the ship's speed only averaged about 18 knots and it was noticeable that she was making rather a lot of smoke.

Our final day at sea proved to be very busy for the ship's tour department as an arrival in Dover the following morning, some three hours later than anticipated, required the rearrangement of a considerable number of travel plans.

Our sailing around the Skaw and southwards through the North Sea was a rather gloomy affair and far more could have been made of our passing of the *Black Watch* which was heading northwards on a Southampton–Norwegian fjords cruise. A rendezvous would certainly have been possible.

With the Dover pilot on board off St Margaret's Bay at 09.40, we waited for a space between the ferry traffic of the *Maersk Dunkerque*, *SeaFrance Moliere* and *Pride of Dover* before passing through the eastern entrance at 10.20 and berthing with the aid of the *DHB Dauntless*, some 20 minutes later.

REFLECTIONS

The *Balmoral* is a beautifully maintained vessel and there was plenty of evidence of ongoing maintenance throughout our cruise. In spite of her age, her paintwork was spotless and the varnished rails and state of her decks were immaculate. It was, however, noted that there was plenty of evidence of soot on Deck 11 around the funnel, especially after a day alongside in port.

Our outside cabin was on the Main Deck – Deck 6 (port side, aft) which was extremely, clean, spacious, quiet and comfortable whilst sleep was never a problem. The bathroom, however, was certainly showing its age with tiles lifting in some places and is it really necessary to fit plastic shower curtains?

Food on board was good and plentiful and it would have been very easy to over eat. The overall standard of food was perhaps four out of five but was

Captain Atle Knutsen on the bridge of the **Balmoral**. *(John Hendy)*

enjoyable and there were plenty of choices at every meal. Our waiters in the Spey Restaurant were polite, friendly, always very helpful and gave excellent service throughout the cruise.

For those readers who have no previous experiences of cruises comes a warning that it is very easy to spend money on board. All sales (shop, bar, wine with meals etc.) are made by use of a credit card which is also used for security purposes when embarking or disembarking and for access to your cabin. Then there is the final day dilemma of how much to tip your cabin stewardess and restaurant waiter. FOCL suggest that £2 per person per day is acceptable but should, in my view, remove this aspect of the cruises from customers. If the company require passengers to subsidise their crew wages then be honest and charge them each a fixed extra amount. It would save so much discussion and concern/stress amongst the passengers and should in theory be easy for the company to implement.

Shore visits are optional and although we planned ours well in advance, some people remained on board, booked theirs during the cruise or simply caught a bus from the cruise terminal into the city. Unless you are with a tour party, visas are required in St Petersburg which again adds to the overall costs but my wife and I each paid in excess of £400 for our shore excursions in addition to £180 on our ship credit cards i.e. an extra £1,000 to the cost of the cruise.

Would we go again? Most certainly, although we might possibly give St Petersburg a miss. This is a shame as it is a beautiful city but there were just too many people and the ordinary cruise passenger is not free to wander at will. One imagines that matters become more acute during July and August.

The whole on-board experience was wonderfully relaxing and escapist. Many of the crew were from the Philippines and south east Asia. They worked long hours, many spending seven months on board before returning home for a two-month break but the vast majority we encountered were helpful, polite and cheerful.

There is an inevitable anti-climax when arriving back in port as passengers rummage for their luggage in the ill-lit baggage hall before boarding a crowded coach to take them to their parked cars. After the comforts of the *Balmoral*, this suddenly brought us down to earth with a jolt. However, as I sit at my desk and type this article, I remain convinced that I could really come to enjoy cruising.

*The bridge of the **Balmoral** whilst alongside in St Petersburg. The main steering console is on the left. (John Hendy)*

The Spey Restaurant (port side aft on Deck 10) was added with the Avon Restaurant (starboard side aft) during the stretching programme in late 1997. They provide excellent views of the sea. (John Hendy)

The SMZ Story

by Henk van der Lugt

The development of the railway network in the Netherlands was relatively slow and it was not until 1872 that Vlissingen was reached where new harbour basins and locks were opened in September 1873. For the first time a port on the Dutch coast was directly connected to the German border by a railway line. This new railway line was operated by the Dutch State Railways (SS)/(Maatschappij tot Exploitatie van Staatsspoorwegen) which in fact was a private company formed to operate railways on Government-built railway lines.

In the years before, a group of Dutch politicians and businessmen had already envisaged the importance of the new railway port of Vlissingen in connection with a shipping line to Britain. This group was strongly supported, not in the least financially, by H.R.H. Prince Hendrik, the younger brother of H.M. King Willem III of the Netherlands.

In October 1874 the group founded a temporary company to start preparations for a shipping line between Vlissingen and a British port.

Three second-hand paddle steamers were acquired. Two of these, *Southern* and *Northern*, had been in use as blockade runners during the American Civil War while the third vessel originally was the first *Snaefell* of the Isle of Man Steam Packet Company. The ships received the names *Stad Middelburg*, *Stad Vlissingen* and *Stad Breda* respectively and were named after towns along the railway line from Vlissingen.

BRITISH INVOLVEMENT

The group came in contact with Mr James Staats Forbes, the general manager of the London, Chatham and Dover Railway (LCDR) who also happened to have business connections in the Netherlands. The LCDR had an agreement with their Kentish rivals the South Eastern Railway (SER) about sharing all revenues from continental services from the Kent coast between Margate and Hastings and Mr Forbes was keen on keeping a possible new continental service outside this agreement. So in negotiations with the new company he offered to build a new pier with railway connection at Queenborough on the River Medway.

During a shareholders meeting on 10th June 1875 it was decided to form the N.V. Stoomvaart Maatschappij Zeeland (SMZ) and the memorandum of association was executed on 22nd June 1875. The traffic agreement between

*The **Stad Middelburg** was S.M.Z.'s first ship and had an earlier career as a blockade runner during the American Civil War. (Henk van der Lugt collection)*

*The **Stad Middelburg** alongside the pontoon in Vlissingen. Not designed for short sea work she appeared to be uneconomical to operate and became reserve ship as soon as specially designed ships became available. (Henk van der Lugt collection)*

Two SMZ vessels alongside the 'T'-shaped Queenborough Pier around 1890. The vessels berthed at the end of the pier, parallel to the shore, while the boat train platform ran the length of the 'neck' of the pier. Closest to the camera is a night boat of the 1878-1883 type while the other vessel is one of the 1887 day boats. (Henk van der Lugt collection)

One of the 1895 night boats alongside Queenborough Pier around 1900.

the SMZ, the SS and the LCDR was signed on 25th June 1875 and the Vlissingen–Sheerness night service was opened on 26th July 1875.

However, all was far from well. The new Queenborough Pier was not ready yet and the ships had to use Sheerness Admiralty Pier where no cargo could be handled. Unfortunately the ships appeared to be rather uneconomic to operate and as the passenger numbers did not come up to expectations, the service was stopped on 14th November for the winter and until the Queenborough Pier was ready for use.

On 15th May 1876 the service was reopened operating to the new Queenborough Pier and on 3rd October that year the Dutch Government gave the first mail contract to the company. Part of this mail contract, however, was the obligation to build two new ships and these entered service in April 1878. They were named *Prinses Marie* and *Prinses Elisabeth* and herewith a long tradition of SMZ ships with Royal names started. Both paddle steamers were built at John Elder & Co's shipyard in Govan. This shipyard (later Fairfield Shipbuilding and Engineering Company) was also to build the next 11 SMZ vessels.

To be able to maintain the service with identical ships, a third vessel was ordered and she entered service as *Prins Hendrik* on 1st July 1880. Meanwhile, in December 1879 the *Stad Vlissingen* had run aground during dense fog. She was refloated, but was so badly damaged that she was scrapped. In 1881 her sister was renamed *Aurora* and refitted for use as reserve vessel but in 1885 she became a coal hulk and she was sold for scrap in 1889.

A fourth new paddle steamer entered service as *Willem, Prins van Oranje* in July 1883. In the previous month the *Stad Breda* had been sold for scrap.

THE DAY SERVICE

Unfortunately the Queenborough Pier was damaged by fire on 18th May 1882 and the ships had to use Dover for passengers and mail while the company had to charter freight ships for a temporary cargo service to London. After about a month Queenborough Pier could be used again although it was not until December 1885 that repairs were completed entirely.

On 7th April 1885 a new mail contract with the Dutch Government was concluded and part of this mail contract was the obligation to start a day service. On 1st June 1887 the day service was opened with the specially built new paddle steamers *Duitschland*, *Engeland* and *Nederland*. They were the first steel-built SMZ ships.

So far SMZ operated the only passenger service between Britain and the Netherlands with connecting (international) trains. This changed on 1st June 1893 when the new railway line to Hoek van Holland was opened. The Harwich–Rotterdam night service of the Great Eastern Railway (GER), which existed since 1863, changed from a local service to an international service as the ships berthed at Hoek van Holland allowing the passengers to transfer to the international trains. These were operated by the Hollandsche IJzeren Spoorweg Maatschappij (HIJSM) and for people travelling from London to Germany via the Netherlands it became possible now to choose between two competing connections, either via Vlissingen with LCDR-SMZ-SS or via Hoek van Holland with GER-HIJSM.

In 1894 the GER introduced three new ships, *Amsterdam*, *Berlin* and *Vienna* and SMZ could only follow with new ships to stay level with their direct competitors. So in 1895 the *Koningin Wilhelmina*, *Koningin Regentes* and *Prins Hendrik* entered the Vlissingen–Queenborough night service. While the new GER ships were screw driven, the new SMZ ships were still paddle steamers. The reason for this appears to be twofold; a conservative SMZ management

One of the 1887 day boats alongside Queenborough Pier, while the handling of cargo or luggage from the train indicates that the ship is being prepared for departure. (Henk van der Lugt collection)

and fears for draught problems in the Medway as screw steamers have a larger draught than paddle steamers of the same size.

The first *Prins Hendrik* was laid up and eventually sold for scrap in 1902 meaning that between 1895 and 1902, SMZ owned two vessels with the name *Prins Hendrik*. It is doubtful, however, if both vessels were ever in service together.

The *Willem, Prins van Oranje* returned to Fairfield's in 1896 to be fitted with new boilers and she became the company's reserve steamer. In 1898 both the *Prinses Elisabeth* and *Prinses Marie* were sold for further use in the Baltic.

In December 1897, very heavy weather damaged the Queenborough branch railway resulting in a temporary shift of the service to Dover.

Of a more severe nature was the disruption of the services after a fire destroyed the Queenborough Pier on 19th July 1900. The SMZ ships now used Port Victoria on the Isle of Grain opposite Queenborough. Originally a SER port, Port Victoria was available now as in 1899 LCDR and SER had formed a working union to become the South Eastern & Chatham Railway Company (SE&CR). After temporary repairs the day service returned to Queenborough in January 1901. The night service, however, could not return until 3rd May 1904 after the Queenborough Pier had been almost completely rebuilt. In the meantime a freight service with chartered steamers had to be operated to Tilbury.

In June 1908 a new mail contract with the Dutch Government was concluded and part of this was the obligation to have three new night boats in service by 1st October 1911. SMZ, however, was anxious to have these vessels in service earlier as at the end of 1907 the GER had introduced a new turbine steamer, the *Copenhagen*, on the Hoek van Holland service. A sister ship, the *Munich*, was delivered in 1908.

SCREW-DRIVEN STEAMERS

The new *Prinses Juliana*, *Oranje Nassau* and *Mecklenburg* were delivered in September, November and December 1909 respectively. They were the last SMZ vessels to be built at Fairfield's and the first screw-driven SMZ vessels. Although there were already several turbine steamers in service on the short sea routes between Britain and the continent, SMZ opted to fit their new steamers with reciprocating engines. Interestingly the vessels did not enter service until April 1910 as the panelling in the public rooms and cabins was fitted by the Dutch firm H.P. Mutters & Zn. after the vessels had arrived in Vlissingen.

After the three new vessels had entered service the three 'old' night steamers were converted for use in the day service. Of the three original day boats the *Engeland* and *Nederland* were scrapped in 1911 while the *Duitschland* became SMZ's reserve steamer. The former reserve steamer, *Willem, Prins van Oranje*, was sold for scrap in 1909.

Negotiations on the 1911 railway timetable between GER, HIJSM and German Railways resulted in an acceleration in transit time from London to Northern Germany via Hoek van Holland of 2 hours. SMZ could only match this by a shorter crossing time. Hence the night service was transferred from

Queenborough to Folkestone on 29th April 1911 thus reducing the distance from 112 to 92 nautical miles.

At the outbreak of the First World War, SMZ had to suspend both services. Later it became possible to maintain a more or less regular service again although Tilbury Docks and eventually Gravesend Pier became the port of call after Folkestone and Queenborough had been closed for SMZ.

Apart from the company's first years, the funnels of the SMZ ships had always been buff with a black top although the width of the black top had been changed a few times. In 1915 narrow red, white and blue bands were added immediately below the black top to indicate the Dutch nationality of the ships. In addition, the ship's name and home port were painted on the hull in large letters.

In 1916 SMZ lost the *Prinses Juliana*, *Mecklenburg* and *Koningin Wilhelmina* which all hit mines laid by the Germans. The remaining screw steamer *Oranje Nassau* was laid up for the rest of the war and from now on an irregular service to Gravesend was maintained by the paddle steamers. The old *Duitschland* was renamed *Zeeland* to emphasise the ship's neutrality. The *Koningin Regentes* was captured by German gunboats and taken to Zeebrugge but released later. The *Prins Hendrik* befell the same fate twice.

Before the war had ended, SMZ had contacted Fairfield's for building identical replacements for both screw steamers but being fully engaged they were not able to build them. SMZ could buy the drawings, however, and ordered two replacements at 'De Schelde' shipyards in Vlissingen instead. The

use of the original drawings explains why SMZ introduced fast cross-channel steamers with piston engines after WW1 when most similar ships were fitted with turbines.

On 1st February 1917 Germany proclaimed the unlimited U-boat war and the service was suspended on this date by order of the Dutch Government and not restarted until after the war.

INTER WAR

From early January 1918 there was an exchange of wounded prisoners of war between Rotterdam and Boston (Lincolnshire). The *Sindoro* of the Rotterdam Lloyd, and the SMZ ships *Zeeland* and *Koningin Regentes* were used for this task but unfortunately the latter was torpedoed on 6th June 1918 near Leman Bank with a loss of seven of those on board.

After the war SMZ reopened the night service on 31st January 1919 with the remaining ships, *Oranje Nassau*, *Prins Hendrik* and *Zeeland*. This firstly operated to Gravesend but in June 1919 reverted to Folkestone.

After lengthy delays, caused by a shortage of materials, the second *Prinses Juliana* which had been ordered during the war, was delivered in August 1920 by 'De Schelde' shipyards. In the same year GER restarted the Hoek van Holland service which resulted in a renewed competition but SMZ did not have an allied railway company in the Netherlands anymore as during the war the two Dutch railway companies SS and HIJSM had merged and became the

*The first **Mecklenburg** arriving at Folkestone around 1912. In the background a South Eastern & Chatham Railway cargo vessel awaits departure for Boulogne. (Henk van der Lugt collection)*

The first **Mecklenburg** arriving at Folkestone after the night service had been transferred from Queenborough in April 1911 reducing the distance from 112 to 92 nautical miles. Apparently the ship arrived with a considerable speed as it looks like the engines are running full astern to kill the speed. (Henk van der Lugt collection)

The **Prins Hendrik** at full speed seen after the restarting of the service on 31st January 1919 when S.M.Z. had to keep the service going with their remaining fleet. This consisted of the screw steamer **Oranje Nassau** and the ageing paddle steamers **Zeeland** (ex **Duitschland**) and **Prins Hendrik**; the latter two were sold for scrap in 1922. (Henk van der Lugt collection)

state-owned Nederlandsche Spoorwegen (NS).

Through the years SS had become a majority shareholder in SMZ and at the merger their shares came into the hands of the Dutch Government which appointed a Government representative to the board of directors.

These were difficult years for SMZ anyway because of a heavy financial burden caused by high interest rates. Besides, traffic numbers did not come up to expectations and it looked as if the other newbuilding, the second *Mecklenburg*, might not be finished.

Messrs Wm. H. Muller & Co, the operators of the Batavier Line, were prepared to give financial support and were appointed managing directors of SMZ in return. The *Mecklenburg* was now completed and entered service in July 1922. The last two paddle steamers *Zeeland* and *Prins Hendrik* were duly sold for scrap in November 1922.

The new Dutch railway company had to run boat trains to the night services of both routes and already in 1921 proposed a move from Vlissingen to Hoek van Holland. This proposal was unacceptable for SMZ but another solution was found as on 1st June 1922, SMZ replaced the night service with a day service. Separate night and day services between the Netherlands and Britain were reinstated now albeit on different routes.

In the mid 1920s the transport of fresh meat (mainly pork) assumed enormous proportions. SMZ owned their own abattoir in Vlissingen and the meat was carried in wooden crates without any refrigeration. In June 1926 Britain forbade the import of fresh meat which proved disastrous for SMZ and eventually led to the end of the agreement with the Southern Railway (SR), the successor of the LC&DR and SE&CR.

A new pooling agreement with the London North Eastern Railway (LNER), the successor of the GER, was concluded. This resulted in a transfer from Folkestone to Harwich on 1st January 1927 and from now on Harwich had a night service to Hoek van Holland and a day service to Vlissingen. Competition had become cooperation!

WORLD WAR TWO

In December 1937 two new motor ships were ordered at 'De Schelde' shipyards. The first ship *Koningin Emma* entered service on 4th June 1939; her sister *Prinses Beatrix* on 3rd July. Only a few months after their introduction the Second World War broke out and the service was suspended. Later, a fairly regular service to Tilbury was maintained by the *Oranje Nassau* but this was halted on 25th

*The **Oranje Nassau** departing from Vlissingen after the rearrangement of the aft two lifeboats in 1931. On all three S.M.Z. steamers the sheltered spaces ahead and astern of the aft hatch were so created, respectively for 1st and 2nd class passengers. (Henk van der Lugt collection)*

*In 1920 a new **Prinses Juliana** entered service, built to the original drawings of her namesake which was lost during the First World War. The ship is pictured before the 1931 rearrangement of the aft two lifeboats on all three SMZ steamers which provided more covered deck space for the passengers. (Henk van der Lugt collection)*

November after which the entire SMZ fleet was laid up in Vlissingen.

After the invasion of the Netherlands on 10th May 1940, the *Koningin Emma*, *Prinses Beatrix*, *Mecklenburg* and *Oranje Nassau* crossed to the Downs, off Deal. The *Prinses Juliana* was requisitioned by the Royal Netherlands Navy to transport troops to IJmuiden but was later bombed by German aircraft off Hoek van Holland and beached. The wreck was later used as a target by the German invaders.

Both steamers were used as accommodation vessels for the Royal Netherlands Navy in various British ports. The *Oranje Nassau* continued in the role for the duration of the war but the *Mecklenburg* was converted into a Landing Ship Infantry (LSI) in 1943 and as such took part in the D-day landings. Both motor ships were requisitioned by the Admiralty, converted beyond recognition into LSIs and flew the White Ensign as HMS *Queen Emma* and HMS *Princess Beatrix*. As such they saw service among others in the Lofoten Islands (Norway), Freetown, Dieppe, the Mediterranean and the Far East. They were not released to SMZ until April 1946.

On her return to the Netherlands on 20th August 1945 *Oranje Nassau* was put on the Dutch Government service between Rotterdam and London and later Harwich where she joined the *Batavier II* of Batavier Line. This service was used by Dutch Government staff, military, etc. On 20th November they were joined by *Mecklenburg* and on 1st July 1946 the *Oranje Nassau* was replaced by *Prinses Beatrix*, the latter still in LSI configuration. The Government service ended in late September 1946.

After being released by the Government *Oranje Nassau* received a short overhaul and on 29th July 1946 she joined LNER's *Prague* on the Harwich–Hoek van Holland night service which became daily except Sundays from then on. The *Prague* had reopened this service on 14th November 1945 on a thrice-weekly basis.

The *Mecklenburg* was released by the Government in early April 1946. After an extensive overhaul, she reopened the day service to Harwich on 14th June 1947 on a thrice-weekly basis. As the port infrastructure in Vlissingen was severely damaged during the war her Dutch port was switched to Hoek van Holland and in the end this was to become the home of SMZ.

DAY SERVICE

On 31st May 1948, the Hoek van Holland–Harwich day service became daily again after the extensive rebuilding and refurbishment of both motor

The **Oranje Nassau** *pictured after the rearrangement of the aft two lifeboats in 1931. When the motor ships entered service in 1939 she was 30 years old and was likely to be sold or scrapped but the outbreak of the Second World War gave her an extra lease of life of 15 years. (G.R. van Veldhoven collection)*

In summer 1939 S.M.Z. introduced their first motor ships **Koningin Emma** *(pictured) and* **Prinses Beatrix**. *After only a few months in service the sister ships had to be laid up due to the outbreak of the Second World War. Both vessels escaped to Britain in May 1940 after which they were converted into Landing Ship Infantry. (Henk van der Lugt collection)*

The **Koningin Emma**, *departing in the day service from Hoek van Holland to Harwich in 1954. In the background is the* **Amsterdam** *of the British Railways night service. (Henk van der Lugt collection)*

The **Koningin Emma** *at sea in the 1960s. At that time she shared the Hoek van Holland - Harwich day service with her sister* **Prinses Beatrix** *and with S.M.Z.'s last conventional vessel, the* **Koningin Wilhelmina**, *which entered service in 1960. Two ships worked the rather relaxed schedule which consisted of a 6 hour crossing followed by 18 hours in port while the third ship was at the S.M.Z. workshops in Vlissingen for lay by and overhaul or was used to duplicate sailings in the summer season. Notice the railway containers on the foredeck. (Henk van der Lugt collection)*

*In February 1960 S.M.Z.'s second **Koningin Wilhelmina**, entered service. She had capacity for around 60 cars which still had to be loaded by crane. Time probably was not yet ready for a car ferry and besides, operating a car ferry in a schedule with two conventional vessels would probably have been difficult. (Henk van der Lugt collection)*

ships had been completed by their builders.

To provide extra capacity on their Rotterdam–Tilbury service the Batavier Line chartered the *Koningin Emma* during the summer of 1948 and the *Oranje Nassau* during the following four summers. Between 1949 and 1952 SMZ ran a twice-weekly summer tourist service between Vlissingen and Folkestone with *Mecklenburg*. As this service was not successful it was not repeated after 1952, neither was the Batavier Line charter.

From now on both motor ships and the *Mecklenburg* shared the day service and sailed to Vlissingen in turn for lay by and overhaul after SMZ had opened a new workshop there in March 1951. The *Oranje Nassau* was sold for scrap in July 1954 after a career of 45 years.

A new motor ship, *Koningin Wilhelmina*, was built by 'De Merwede' Shipyards in Hardinxveld-Giessendam. She made her maiden voyage on 7th February 1960 and replaced the *Mecklenburg* which was sold for scrap in May 1960, when 38 years old. The new ship had a capacity for 60 motor cars but these still had to be loaded by crane.

CAR TRAFFIC

In the 1960s demand for car space increased and SMZ and British Railways (the successor of LNER) decided to reorganise their services and each ordered a new drive on–drive off car ferry. Both the new British car ferry, *St. George*, and the new SMZ car ferry, *Koningin Juliana*, entered service in 1968 although the latter was delayed by a fire while fitting out at her builders, Cammell Laird in Birkenhead. The schedules were integrated and the SMZ ship worked the day service from Hoek van Holland and returned in the night service while the British ship worked opposite her. The 1939 motor ships were sold for breaking up in late 1968 while the *Koningin Wilhelmina* was only used to provide extra sailings in the summer season and was laid up in Vlissingen for the rest of the year.

Between 1968 and 1972, SMZ operated a container service between Rotterdam and Harwich in cooperation with British Railways. SMZ's contribution was the containership *Domburgh* of Wm. H. Muller & Co which

was later replaced by chartered ships.

A third car ferry, *St. Edmund*, was introduced by the British partners early in 1975 and in 1978 the route's fourth car ferry, *Prinses Beatrix*, was delivered to SMZ by the Verolme Shipyards in Heusden. After her arrival *Koningin Wilhelmina* was sold for further use in the Mediterranean. The workshop in Vlissingen was closed now and thus SMZ's last link with Vlissingen was severed.

In 1983 both British ships were replaced by the huge *St. Nicholas*, chartered from the Swedish Stena Line. SMZ decided to make a similar move and ordered a large ferry at Van der Giessen – de Noord in Krimpen aan den IJssel.

In order to enlarge the capacity in anticipation of the new ship, SMZ chartered the Norwegian *Peter Wessel* from Larvik Line from 1984 until 1986. She was renamed *Zeeland*, flew the Dutch flag and replaced the *Koningin Juliana* which was sold to become an exhibition ship to promote Dutch exports. As this fell through she saw further service in the Mediterranean.

On 1st October 1985 the *Prinses Beatrix* was sold to Brittany Ferries and chartered back under the French flag until the introduction of the new *Koningin Beatrix* on 22nd April 1986.

SMZ was 70% state owned and in 1988 the Minister of Transport and Public Works announced that the Dutch Government intended to sell its controlling interest in the company. In anticipation of the privatisation SMZ marketed itself as Crown Line and the ship's livery was adjusted accordingly.

Out of four prospective buyers the Swedish Stena Line emerged as winner. The official transfer of SMZ to Stena Line took place on board the *Koningin Beatrix* on 22nd June 1989.

So after 114 years came an end to one of the oldest Dutch shipping companies which encountered highs and lows but which always provided a reliable service.

The **Koningin Juliana** alongside at Hoek van Holland in June 1978, while a brand new **Prinses Beatrix** is passing, underway from the shipyard for sea trials. Notice the two gangways on **Koningin Juliana**; one for the 1st class and one for the 2nd class passengers. (G.R. van Veldhoven)

S.M.Z.'s last ship, the **Koningin Beatrix**, entered service in April 1986. Early in 1989 the ship's livery was changed as S.M.Z. marketed itself as Crown Line prior to the privatisation of the company. On 22nd June 1989 the official transfer of S.M.Z. to Stena Line took place on board the ship whilst alongside at Hoek van Holland. (Henk van der Lugt collection)

3 Photo Feature - Ferries of the Irish Sea
by Miles Cowsill and Gordon Hislip

*The **European Endeavour** was chartered by DFDS in August 2010 to cover for the refits of the company on the Irish Sea. The P&O vessel is pictured here at the DFDS terminal at Dublin. (Gordon Hislip)*

The **Stena Caledonia** was built in 1981 for Sealink as the **St. David** for the Fishguard–Rosslare service but with the success of the **Stena Normandica** on the route she was placed initially on the Holyhead–Dun Laoghaire link. At the age of 30 years, she is now the oldest ferry on the Irish Sea but with the extensive refurbishment work that Stena Line have undertaken in recent years she remains in immaculate order and she is due to remain in service until at least 2012 when the new port at Cairnryan opens. (Gordon Hislip)

Built originally for SNCF as the **Champs Elysees**, she saw service not only at Calais but also at Dieppe prior to moving to the Stranraer–Larne service in 2009. She was renamed the **SeaFrance Manet** in 1997 but became redundant in 2008 and was purchased by Stena Line to support the **Stena Caledonia** following the reduction of sailings of the HSS craft **Stena Voyager** due to spiralling worldwide oil costs. (Gordon Hislip)

*DFDS Seaways' newly-painted **Scotia Seaways** leaving Dublin for Heysham. All the former Norfolk Line fleet were repainted during summer 2010 in new livery and all the original fleet were completely renamed by their new Danish owners. (Gordon Hislip)*

*The **Ben-my-Chree** arrives at Douglas on one of her regular sailings from Heysham. The vessel has operated over 1.076 million nautical miles (43 times around the world) since she came into service in 1998. Her near sister the **Commodore Clipper** operates the Channel Islands operations for Condor Ferries but her accommodation is far superior to that of the Manx vessel. (Miles Cowsill)*

In the next couple of years Stena Line will have to decide on what replacement tonnage will be put on the Fleetwood–Larne service as the current vessels from P&O's former fleet are now beginning to show their age in spite of extensive refurbishment since the Swedish company took over the service in 2004. The **Stena Leader** *is pictured here leaving Larne on her seven-hour crossing to Fleetwood. (Gordon Hislip)*

The **European Mariner** *maintains P&O Ferries' Larne-Troon service. In spite of heavy competition on all Irish Sea routes during the last five years, this route continues to attract good loads of traffic. The German-built ship has seen various owners during her career and now is one of the oldest freight vessels on the Irish Sea, having been built some 33 years ago. (Miles Cowsill)*

In 2001, Irish Ferries introduced the Finnish-built **Ulysses** on the Holyhead–Dublin service. With capacity for 1,785 passengers and 1,342 cars or 300 lorries she has held the accolade of being the largest ferry in the world. With the introduction of the new **Stena Hollandica** and **Stena Britannica** on the North Sea in 2010 she will no longer be the largest ferry operating. (Miles Cowsill)

Built originally in Japan for P&O Irish Sea as the **Stena Ambassador**, her career on the Liverpool–Dublin and Mostyn service was to be short lived before the vessel was sold to Stena Line in 2004. After her sale she was transferred to the Karlskrona–Gdynia service and renamed **Stena Nordica**. Some four years later she returned to the Irish Sea as an important strategic operator with the **Stena Adventurer** on the Holyhead–Dublin route. (Gordon Hislip)

The Italian-built **Lagan Seaways** maintains the Liverpool-Belfast service. She is seen here outward bound from Belfast following receiving her new DFDS livery and renaming. The Liverpool-Belfast service continues to be a successful service for the company on its nine-hour passage on the Irish Sea. (Gordon Hislip)

In 1996 the **Stena Explorer** made her debut on the Irish Sea as a new future generation of travel concept. The continued spiralling oil prices during the last decade have made her and her two sisters uneconomic to operate against conventional shipping. For 2010 the vessel was only employed for eight weeks and her near sister the **Stena Voyager** has operated reduced sailings on the North Channel. The Dutch-based **Stena Discovery** was sold in 2009 to Venezuelan interests, where as one of the principal oil nations oil costs are not a problem. (Gordon Hislip)

The **Norbay** and **Norbank** (pictured here) were built for the Hull–Rotterdam service to support the **Norsun** and **Norsea** with the expanding growth in traffic between the UK and Northern Europe. In January 2002 both sisters were transferred to the Liverpool–Dublin route and operate in tandem, together offering most days two round sailings from each port. (Miles Cowsill)

The **Clipper Pace** was built in Spain in a series of six vessels for the Clipper Group. The first of the delayed vessels, the **Clipper Point**, came into service in 2008 and she was subsequently joined by the **Clipper Pace**, **Clipper Panorama** and **Clipper Pennant**. A further two ships were due to follow but the Clipper Group cancelled their construction following all the delays with the first four vessels. (Gordon Hislip)

The introduction of the **Express** on the Irish Sea in 2005 has brought reliability of service to P&O Ferries' operations on their Larne–Cairnryan/Troon services. Originally built for Buquebus of Argentina as the **Catelonia 1** between Barcelona and Mallorca in 2000 she was chartered to P&O and renamed **Portsmouth Express** to offer increased capacity on the Portsmouth–Cherbourg link. Following the demise of P&O's operations at Portsmouth she was renamed **Katelonia** before returning to the company on a long-term charter. (Miles Cowsill)

The introduction of the **European Causeway** and the **European Highlander** (pictured here) brought an overnight success for P&O on their Larne–Cairnryan route. Not only have both ships proved extremely popular with the travelling public and freight hauliers, they have also proved to be very reliable on their 105-minute crossings between Scotland and Ireland. With capacity for 410 passengers and 315 cars they brought increased capacity to the route in place of the former jumboised 'Free Enterprise' class ships. (Miles Cowsill)

*Built as the **Kronprinsessan Victoria** for the Gothenburg–Frederikshavn service for Sessan Line, shortly after her delivery the company was taken over by Stena Line. After operating various routes in the Baltic in 1998 she was renamed the **Stena Europe** for the Fishguard–Rosslare route. The vessel has remained on the route for the last eight years operating in tandem during the peak season with the **Stena Lynx III**. (Gordon Hislip)*

*The **Norman Voyager** arrives at Rosslare from Cherbourg. The vessel, originally built in Italy, was acquired by LD Lines for their Portsmouth-Le Havre route but in 2009, in a surprise move she was chartered to Celtic Link to enable them to expand and improve their service between Ireland and France. (Gordon Hislip)*

In March 2010 Fastnet Line re-established the Swansea–Cork service with the former **Olau Britannia**. The former Olau and Color Line ship was acquired from the Finnish Bank following the demise of a short-lived service between Helsinki and St Petersburg when Color Line sold her. The new link got off to a poor start and in light of the current economic climate and severe competition for traffic on the Irish Sea, it will be interesting to see how the service develops. (Fastnet Line)

The **Pont-Aven** makes a weekly call at the port of Cork during her busy schedules as part of Brittany Ferries' extensive web of operations on the western seaboard of Britain, France, Ireland and Spain. She has proved extremely popular since her introduction in 2003 and runs in competition to Irish Ferries' service from Rosslare with the **Oscar Wilde**. (Miles Cowsill)

4 The Superfast Series

by Richard Seville

When newcomer Superfast Ferries burst onto the Adriatic in 1995, with a pair of high-speed cruise ferries in Ferrari red livery, their arrival was literally revolutionary. Prior to their debut, it had been over 30 years since newbuild tonnage had been commissioned by Greek operators for the Italy to Greece routes, with the majority of companies operating converted second-hand vessels. Whilst some of these conversions were undoubtedly impressive, one key theme was that the speed of these ships was usually rather pedestrian. The longer routes, principally from Ancona or Venice, would therefore take upwards of 40 hours on passage, and necessitate two nights on board. In the early 1990s, speeds began to increase with the dominant operators, Minoan Lines in particular, introducing faster vessels. However, it was the arrival of Superfast which accelerated progress in this area, with the new twins *Superfast I* and *Superfast II* they were able to complete the voyage to Patras in less than 24 hours, whilst offering stylish modern facilities that set new standards in the region. From the moment of their debut, Superfast became an astonishing success, rapidly expanding to the extent that within seven years, no fewer than 12 new ferries had been commissioned, for a route network which included the Adriatic, the Baltic and North Sea.

THE BRAND

The Superfast brand was the idea of Pericles Panagopulos, who had previously founded and run the upmarket Royal Cruise Line. Having sold this business, Panagopulos saw an opportunity in the Adriatic trades, which were booming due to the conflict in the Balkans having closed the overland route to Greece and beyond. An order was placed in 1993 with the Schichau shipyard in Bremen, Germany for two sister vessels, with capacity for 1,410 passengers, 200 cabins, and vehicle decks accommodating up to 830 cars. Most notable, however, was their service speed of 27 knots. The inaugural route was launched between Patras and Ancona on 6th April 1995, with the second vessel entering service to double capacity and offer daily departures just two months later. Of the main incumbent operators, Minoan, ANEK and Strintzis, only Minoan had any ferry capable of rivalling this new upstart. Their first ever newbuild, the *Arethusa*, was delivered slightly earlier, but was hindered by a service speed of 23 knots and of course, the remainder of the fleet was unable to match this, meaning only irregular departures could be offered.

Unsurprisingly, backed by impressive marketing, Superfast made significant inroads into the market, and soon established themselves as the premier company on the Adriatic. Expansion was swift, and July 1996 saw a further two sister vessels ordered for delivery in 1998, with similar passenger capacity, but a larger garage and even faster speed at 28.5 knots. Their arrival from Kvaerner Masa, Turku, allowed a second route to open between Bari and Patras, operated by the cascaded initial twins.

Just three months after the delivery of the *Superfast III* and 'IV', orders were announced for four further vessels, with an option for an additional two, all from Howaldtswerke-Deutsche Werft, Kiel. The confirmed order comprised two different designs, the first pair being larger evolutions of the previous sisters, but the second pair (and the options) being of an entirely different design, with a smaller passenger capacity of just 717 passengers, although the speed, and external appearance, were clearly of the Superfast lineage. *Superfast V* and 'VI' were to join the original service between Patras and Ancona but the subsequent quartet were destined to launch Superfast's expansion in the Baltic.

In May 2001, the first of this quartet, the *Superfast VII* began operations between Rostock and Hanko, close to Helsinki, and was soon joined by her sister. The third sister of this quartet then inaugurated a service between Rostock and Sodertalje, south of Stockholm, in January 2002, although this was to prove short lived. Despite significant local investment, this service closed in May 2002, when the *Superfast IX* was transferred to the North Sea to open a route between Rosyth and Zeebrugge, Belgium, where she was joined by the fourth sister, the *Superfast X*. While the six vessels from Kiel had been under construction, astonishingly, a further set of twins had been ordered from Flender Werft, Lubeck, for the original route, carrying 1,439 passengers, up to 653 cars, and with a speed of 29.2 knots. During the course of the delivery of the Superfast series, the company had also taken over Greek rival Strintzis Lines, which was rebranded as Blue Star Ferries. Both this business and Superfast Ferries subsequently became subsidiaries of a new holding company, Attica Enterprises.

ACCOMMODATION

Throughout the entire series of 12 vessels, in order to portray the powerful Superfast brand, there was a clear family external appearance, particularly in the striking winged funnel. There was also a consistent company interior design/decor, and when studying the series, it is clear how the actual layout design evolved over time. The first twins had relatively small public accommodation, concentrated on one level, Deck 7. Flow was principally through a narrow starboard-side arcade, which commenced at the top of the stern escalator from the vehicle decks. Passengers entered into an open plan arcade bar, which led to port to the main show bar and from there forward into the cafeteria. On the starboard side, the arcade continued forward, passing a small à la carte restaurant, the reception area, and two duty-free shops. Two recliner lounges were located to starboard, whilst cabin accommodation occupied the forward section and the entirety of Deck 8 above. Astern at this level was a sheltered lido and pool area.

In vessels 'III' and 'IV', the design evolved to create parallel arcades on either beam on the main deck, each passing through open plan restaurant/cafeteria areas to an additional bar forward, whilst a more spacious Lido area was housed forward of the funnel. The layout on 'V' and 'VI' was highly similar, but with a more impressive twin-level bar astern.

The next quartet were an entirely different proposition, with far simpler public accommodation suited to their smaller passenger capacity, albeit outfitted in the identical corporate style. These vessels shared a large lounge

*The first of the 12-strong series was the **Superfast I,** seen here at Patras. (Miles Cowsill)*

*Also seen at Patras is her twin, the **Superfast II**. The sisters inaugurated Superfast's operations on the Adriatic in 1995. (Miles Cowsill)*

The **Superfast XII**, the final vessel in the series, is pictured at Heraklion, preparing to depart for Piraeus, the route she has served since 2009. (Richard Seville)

Captured at Patras is one of the largest ferries in the series, the **Superfast V**, now Brittany Ferries' **Cap Finistere**. (John Hendy)

bar forward, which led aft through reception and shopping areas into an open plan cafeteria, with a central aperitif bar and separate à la carte restaurant area. Whilst lacking an external pool, which was entirely in line with their Northern operating environment, the four did boast a small spa complex on the uppermost passenger deck. The final duo were clearly evolved from the preceding quartet rather than the 'V' and 'VI', as they also offered lounge bars forward on the main deck, which had not been previously seen in the Adriatic ships. Facilities led astern through the catering outlets to a further bar aft, without the twin levels. The main Lido area was again located forward of the funnel.

CONTRACTION

Initially, when the early Superfast vessels were displaced by the latest stream of newbuilds, they were used to expand the network; however, subsequently, many of the vessels have become available for sale. This process has been accelerated with the contraction of the route network from its peak in 2002, and today, only three of the original 12 passenger vessels remain under Greek ownership, although these have admittedly been augmented by the ro-pax sisters, the second *Superfast I* and 'II'.

Unsurprisingly, when made available for sale, with their quality construction, comfortable accommodation and high speed, the Superfast ferries were in high demand. The first to leave the fleet were not 'I' and 'II', but rather the 'III' and 'IV'. They were acquired in 2002 by the Australian TT-Line, to replace their *Spirit of Tasmania* of 1986.

As the *Spirit of Tasmania I* and *Spirit of Tasmania II*, they partner on the overnight link between Melbourne and Devonport, Tasmania, and remain relatively unaltered internally, with the duty-free shops now Tourism Offices. Externally, the swimming pools have been covered over, and the enclosure of the sheltered deck area aft on Deck 9 is to become a fully fledged lounge area. It is also interesting to note, however, that Superfast initially mandated the removal of the funnel wingtips, judging this to be a trademark – a practice which has subsequently lapsed. Enjoying significant early success, they were joined in late 2003 by the former *Superfast II*, renamed the *Spirit of Tasmania III* to relaunch the longer connection to Sydney. Although inaugurated with great fanfare, and spectacular images of the vessel sailing beneath the iconic Sydney Harbour Bridge, the secondary route quickly failed to establish profitability and was axed in late 2006.

The *Spirit of Tasmania III* was sold to Corsica Ferries, and was significantly

*Gathering speed as she heads out of Piraeus, the **Superfast XII** is seen from an inbound Salamis ferry in June 2009. (Richard Seville)*

rebuilt at Perama prior to a third career as the *Mega Express Four*. The main change during her Australian service had been the removal of the pool aft on Deck 8, and the creation of the so-called Southern Cross Atrium, a semi-enclosed lounge bar. Far greater changes were undertaken by Corsica Ferries, with her superstructure extended right aft, including a panoramic spiral staircase overlooking her stern, in the style of their purpose-built *Mega Express* of 2000. The extension created additional lounge and retail space on Deck 7, a large reception hall and reclining seat lounges on Deck 6, and also allowed for the reinstatement of an outdoor swimming pool astern of the Southern Cross Atrium, which was retained. In addition, the original public room layout on Deck 7 was altered forward, with the duty-free shops and recliner lounges merged to create a large, open plan Spaghetteria.

February 2004 saw the original *Superfast I* acquired by Grimaldi Ferries, to support their recently launched cruise ferry service between Barcelona and Civitavecchia as the *Eurostar Roma*. Her accommodation also remained largely unchanged in this guise, but like her sister, she was to be rebuilt by her third operator, Unity Line. Displaced by purpose-built tonnage in early 2008, she was sold to the Polish company to operate from Swinousjscie and Ystad, Sweden. Renamed *Skania*, her accommodation was extended aft on Deck 8, with an additional bar lounge and conference facilities created in place of the former Lido area, while an awkwardly located recliner lounge was constructed on Deck 9. Otherwise, the layout of her main public rooms on 7

*Now in her third career, the former **Superfast I** is now the Polish **Skania**, shown at an overcast Ystad in May 2010. (Richard Seville)*

*Left to maintain the Rosyth to Zeebrugge service alone after the dispatch of her sister to the Baltic, the **Superfast X** is shown arriving at the Belgian port. (Mike Louagie)*

One of only two of the series remaining on the Adriatic in 2010, the **Superfast XI** *swings as she approaches Igoumenitsa in 2008. (Richard Seville)*

The **Superfast VIII** *photographed in Tallink livery whilst berthed in the Estonian capital during January 2008. (Richard Seville)*

*En route to her new career in eastern Canada, the former **Superfast IX** is pictured as Marine Atlantic's **Atlantic Vision**. (FotoFlite)*

*Having been converted for short sea service, the one-time **Superfast X** is shown off at Calais as the **SeaFrance Moliere**. (John Hendy)*

The **Superfast V** was delivered to Brittany Ferries in early 2010 to allow the company to expand the operations to Spain. The former Greek vessel is pictured here as the **Cap Finistere** en route to Spain from Portsmouth. (FotoFlite)

Now serving on the opposite side of the globe, the **Spirit of Tasmania II** *was originally the Finnish built* **Superfast IV**. *(Brian Smith)*

Clearly showing her significant aft extension, the **Mega Express Four** *heads away from Toulon in late September 2007. (Richard Seville)*

deck is as built, with some facilities, such as the Berlin Bar, even retaining their Superfast names.

All four of the smaller quartet have also now left the Superfast fleet. After the closure of the Swedish route, operations settled down with the 'VII' and 'VIII' on the Germany to Finland service, while the 'IX' and 'X' ran between Scotland and Belgium. The first change occurred in November 2005, when the 'IX' was removed from the North Sea and transferred to join her sisters in the Baltic. Shortly afterwards, in April 2006, this route and the three sisters serving it were all sold to Tallink, which eventually resulted in the transfer of the Finnish terminal to Helsinki itself, although the ships were not renamed. Superfast initially continued to maintain a freight-only presence in the Baltic, although this has since ceased.

SEAFRANCE, TALLINK AND BRITTANY FERRIES

The Rosyth to Zeebrugge route soldiered on with the *Superfast X* alone until February 2007, when she was replaced by the *Blue Star 1* and sold to SNCM. Renamed the *Jean Nicoli*, she was purchased to bolster their fleet, and

image, at a time when their core Corsican routes were out to tender and they were facing an aggressive bid from Corsica Ferries. She never saw actual service for SNCM, for once the tender had been won, she was instead chartered out to ANEK Lines for service between Italy and Greece. By the end of the year, declared surplus to requirements, she had been sold to SeaFrance for conversion to serve between Dover and Calais.

If the conversion of a long-distance overnight ferry for a 90-minute shuttle route was ill conceived, the execution was poorer still. During her rebuild at Dunkirk, cabins were removed from her Deck 8 to create an enlarged duty-free shop forward and new lounge bar midships, with an adjacent à la carte restaurant; although the original tiny cabin windows were not replaced. The original saloon deck was surprisingly little altered, save for the conversion of the à la carte restaurant into a truckers' restaurant, the reconfiguration of the buffet restaurant into a self-service cafeteria, the removal of the aperitif bar to increase the seating in this area and the re-upholstering of some soft furnishings in SeaFrance colours. Whilst such a conversion was always going to be challenging, it seems that with further

Seen from the Harbour Bridge, the former **Superfast II** *heads out on passage to Tasmania, on the short lived service from Sydney. Compare her stern with the photo of the rebuilt* **Mega Express Four** *above. (Brian Smith)*

consideration, a far more satisfactory layout could have been achieved.

As the *SeaFrance Moliere*, she made her much delayed debut on the Dover Strait in August 2008, to mixed reviews, and continues to suffer from operational challenges. With much of her cabin accommodation remaining intact, she would seem far better suited to a route of between four and six hours in duration. Shortly after her acquisition, SeaFrance's fortunes significantly worsened – in part certainly attributable to the extensive purchase and overrun conversion costs of the former *Superfast X*. The *SeaFrance Moliere* continues between Dover and Calais at present, as the company teeters on the edge of bankruptcy.

Tallink deployed their three Superfast vessels on Helsinki to Tallinn crossings during layovers between service to Rostock from January 2007 onwards. The future of the lengthy and fuel-thirsty route to Germany has often attracted speculation, and Tallink's actions certainly fuel such comment. In September 2008 the *Superfast IX* was chartered to Marine Atlantic of Canada for their North Sydney to Port-aux-Basques operation. Renamed the *Atlantic Vision* she entered service largely unaltered, and astonishingly, received local criticism that her public facilities were too luxurious! Back in the Baltic, the route has subsequently been reduced to summer-only operation. It seems probable Tallink were hoping for Marine Atlantic to take the remaining twins on charter to complete their fleet renewal, but in June 2010 it emerged they were to convert the *Stena Traveller* and *Stena Trader* for this purpose instead.

A major milestone in the company's history occurred in September 2007 when Pericles Panagopulos sold his participation in Attica to the Marfin Investment Group. His son, Alexander, who had been CEO, had resigned prior to this sale. This change of control was ultimately to see a notable change in direction for the business. When the Superfast route from Rosyth to Zeebrugge was eventually closed in September 2008, the company's presence was again limited to the Adriatic. At this point, all four remaining vessels ... the 'V', 'VI', 'XI' and 'XII' ... were engaged between Patras and Ancona, with the Bari connection having been ceded to subsidiary Blue Star Ferries. In late 2008, the company announced the off-the-shelf acquisition of two ro-pax freighters from an extensive series ordered by Grandi Navi Veloci. With accommodation for just 375 passengers and simple passenger accommodation, these sisters, which assumed the names *Superfast I* and

Superfast II and took over the Patras to Bari route, demonstrated the new direction of the company in distinct contrast to the original ethos. With Panagopulos having left, the emphasis on cruise-style operations ceased. The year 2009 saw further developments, with the *Superfast XII* transferred to the Aegean to inaugurate a new route between Piraeus and Heraklion, Crete, and then, in early 2010, the sale of the *Superfast V* to Brittany Ferries was announced.

Brittany Ferries acquired the 2000-built vessel to bolster their Spanish services, renaming her the *Cap Finistère*. Upon entry into service, she maintains weekend services between Portsmouth and Santander, whilst serving Cherbourg in between. With limited time available to ready her for the 2010 season, Brittany Ferries announced only minor modifications would be made until they had time to assess her in service. As a result, internally, like the *SeaFrance Moliere*, she is instantly recognisable as a Superfast vessel. Indeed, the only major change was the conversion of a previous casino area into a walk-through cafe, and, unusually for the French operator, many references to her Greek operators remain throughout.

ADRIATIC

Since 1995, the Adriatic market has changed considerably, with the reopening of the overland route through the Balkans and the advent of low-cost air travel being just two factors. Today, only three of the original 12 vessels in the series remain in Superfast ownership with only two on the original Adriatic crossing. With the change in ownership, the ethos of the business has significantly changed, and it appears unlikely that any further examples will be built. The 12 ferries represent an astonishing investment and Panagopulos' legacy is a series of high-quality, aesthetically powerful, stylish and comfortable overnight vessels which are now in service literally around the globe. The series remain instantly recognisable through their external and internal design, and travel on any of the vessels is highly recommended.

Vessel	Year Built	Original Tonnage	Passenger/ Vehicle Capacity	Speed	Current Owner	Current Name	Current Route
Superfast I	1995	23, 663	1410/830	27 kn	Unity Line	**Skania**	Ystad - Swinouscjie
Superfast II	1995	23,663	1410/830	27 kn	Corsica Ferries	**Mega Express Four**	Toulon/Nice - Corsica
Superfast III	1998	29,067	1404/1000	28.5 kn	Spirit of Tasmania	**Spirit of Tasmania II**	Melbourne - Devonport
Superfast IV	1998	29,067	1404/1000	28.5 kn	Spirit of Tasmania	**Spirit of Tasmania I**	Melbourne - Devonport
Superfast V	2000	32,728	1608/712	28 kn	Brittany Ferries	**Cap Finistere**	Portsmouth - Santander
Superfast VI	2000	32,728	1608/712	28 kn	Superfast		Patras- Ancona
Superfast VII		30,285	717/653	28.6 kn	Tallink		Helsinki -Rostock
Superfast VIII	2001	30,285	717/653	28.6 kn	Tallink		Helsinki - Rostock
Superfast IX	2002	30,285	717/653	28.6 kn	Tallink (chartered to Marine Atlantic)	**Atlantic Vision**	North Sydney - Port aux Basques
Superfast X	2002	30,285	717/653	28.6 kn	SeaFrance	**SeaFrance Moliere**	Dover - Calais
Superfast XI	2002	30,902	1429/653	29.2 kn	Superfast		Patras - Ancona
Superfast XII	2002	30,902	1429/653	29.2 kn	Superfast		Piraeus - Heraklion

5 Photo Feature - Istanbul
by William Mayes

Istanbul, truly the city where east meets west is unlike anywhere else on earth; the sights, sounds, smells, hustle and bustle of everyday life in the back streets, the daily migration between Asia and Europe on the more than 200 ferries operating in the region serve to make Istanbul unique. The major ferries, numbering around 90 are operated by IDO (Istanbul Sea Buses), a municipal company that is likely to be privatised in the near future. On the basis of the number of passengers carried IDO is the world's largest ferry company, regularly transporting more than 100 million passengers annually. Istanbul, located at the entrance to the Black Sea is now also a very important cruise port, both for transit visits and turn-round calls. What follows is a look at some of the variety of cruise ships that called at the Istanbul cruise terminal in 2008 and 2010.

The **Ankara** is one of three Polish-built vessels delivered to Turkish Maritime Lines in the 1980s for the coastal passenger and car ferry services, and further afield, to Italy. When the company was wound up, the **Ankara** was acquired by Deniz Cruise and Ferry Lines and now operates on the Turkish coast as a ferry and in the Greek islands as a cruise ship.

Heading up through the Bosphorus towards the Black Sea, the **Astoria** is seen in her final season with German operator Transocean Tours. Subsequently both that company, and the ship's owner, Club Cruise of the Netherlands, collapsed and the **Astoria** now sails for Saga as the **Saga Pearl II**.

There are few ships in service that still have an attractive profile, but Fred. Olsen's **Black Watch** is one of them. Built in Finland in 1972 as the **Royal Viking Star**, she was one of the first of the new luxury cruise ships in a relatively immature market. The concept of luxury has changed greatly over the intervening 40 years, and she now serves the mid-range British market.

The **Celebrity Equinox** is the second ship in a series of five being built for Celebrity Cruises by the Meyer shipyard in Papenburg. Celebrity has been operating a number of ships in Europe each summer for many years, and in 2011 is expected to have five ships based in European ports.

Carnival Corporation uses the same basic ship platform across various cruise brands within the Group. The **Costa Serena** is such an example, very similar to the **Carnival Splendor** and a development from the slightly smaller **Carnival Conquest** class. The **Costa Concordia** and **Costa Pacifica** are sisters to the **Costa Serena**.

Below the waterline the **Cristal** consists of parts of the 1980-built **Viking Saga**, two fires and several names later. Following her life as a ferry, she has had a number of cruise roles including Star Cruises' **Superstar Taurus** and NCL's **Leeward**. Following a long lay-up in Tilbury as the **Opera** she passed to Louis Cruises in 2007 as a replacement for the **Sea Diamond** which was lost off Santorini.

As the **Island Princess**, this ship was one of the original Loveboats. Later she operated briefly on cruises from South Korea for Hyundai, but was acquired by Gerry Herrod in 2001 for conversion to a soft expedition ship. The operation was later acquired by All Leisure Group and the ship now operates in the cultural cruise market.

The **Grand Princess** was the first British-owned passenger ship to have a gross tonnage greater than 100,000, although not the world's first as that title goes to the **Carnival Destiny**. The **Grand Princess** design has provided the platform for a further ten ships for P&O Cruises and Princess Cruises, including the former's **Azura** and **Ventura**.

The funnel rather gives the game away that the **Halas** has been around for a while. She actually started sailing as an Istanbul ferry in 1923, having been built in 1915 by Fairfields on the River Clyde. In the intervening years she operated for the Royal Navy as HMS **Waterwitch**, a dispatch vessel. She ceased to be used as a ferry in the mid 1980s and after some years laid up, was converted for use as a luxury cruise ship, sailing the Turkish coasts.

The **MSC Poesia** is the third member of the Orchestra class of four 92,000-gross ton vessels built for the company at St Nazaire. She is shown here during her first season in service. Her sisters are the **MSC Musica, MSC Orchestra** and **MSC Magnifica.**

The old hull on which the rather more modern superstructure of the **Ocean Monarch** sits has given remarkable service to various owners for 55 years, having started as the cargo ship **Port Sydney**. She was recently acquired by Classic International Cruises and now sails under the name **Princess Daphne**.

The **Oriana** was the first purpose-built cruise ship for the British market and was delivered in 1995. She is seen here heading south from the Black Sea port of Odessa, bound for Palma de Majorca and then home to Southampton. Either the **Oriana** or the **Aurora** has made an annual Black Sea cruise since 2001.

The **Queen Victoria** is one of a number of Vista class ships built by Fincantieri and spread through the Carnival Corporation fleets of Costa, Cunard, Holland America and P&O Cruises. Her near sister, the **Queen Elizabeth**, was delivered in October 2010.

Having arrived in the morning from Sochi in Russia, the **Saga Ruby** remained in port until just before midnight, sailing then for Heraklion, Mahon, Gibraltar and Lisbon on her way back to Southampton. She was on a 28-night Black Sea cruise that included calls at Constanta, Varna, Odessa, Yalta and Sevastopol that will be repeated in 2011.

Built in 1931 for Emily Cadwaller, the granddaughter of John Roebling (builder of New York's Brooklyn Bridge), the **Savarona** was sold to the Government of Turkey in 1938 for use as the presidential yacht of Kemal Attaturk. After various roles she was rebuilt as a charter cruise ship, but it is thought that she may become a museum exhibit in the near future.

The **Seven Seas Voyager** is a premium market ship but in today's economic climate, as with all lines, Regent Seven Seas Cruises is feeling the pinch and so it has recently included shore excursions in the basic price. The ship carries around 700 passengers with 450 crew. Regent is now part of the Prestige Cruises division of Apollo Management.

Silversea Cruises is a relative newcomer to the industry, having started trading in 1994, with its first ship, the **Silver Cloud**. The company now operates six ships in the upper premium market, including the soft expedition ship **Prince Albert II**, and has one further ship on order.

The **Fairsky** was the first new ship for Sitmar Line and, although the company had ordered a further three cruise ships, she was also the last as P&O took control of the company before they were delivered. As the **Sky Wonder** she has operated for the Spanish Pullmantur, a subsidiary of Royal Caribbean Cruise Lines for a number of years, but is currently laid up in Marseille as the **Atlantic Star**.

The Cork Connection

by Matthew Punter

One of the defining characteristics of the modern vehicle ferry era is the number of inherently marginal services that manage to wring out something of an existence around the British Isles. Whilst the aviation industry has made a virtue out of serving increasingly esoteric destinations over the last two decades, the dominant thrust of the short-sea operators has been to consolidate around a diminishing number of core services. This process has been accelerated by the triple whammy of the loss of duty free, the huge rise in low-cost flight networks and more recently the economic recession. Of course, none of these have precipitated a collapse in the ferry networks around our island; just a sad, steady attrition in ships and routes as the years roll on and Darwinian principles take hold in the ferry industry.

Many historic services have vanished in recent years from the route maps of the British ferry scene: Folkestone–Boulogne, Felixstowe–Zeebrugge, Harwich–Hamburg, Newcastle–Bergen and this year Poole–Cherbourg, with a 'proper' ferry at least. Yet what distinguishes the ferry industry from its aeronautical equivalent is the discernible sense of loss that appears to be felt by the communities previously served by a ferry. Ferry routes are intrinsically linked to the physical geographies of our coastline. This frequently leaves diminutive small communities such as Harwich or Fishguard somewhat over-dependent on the vast leviathans that disgorge fleeting travellers into their midst whilst providing a source of employment and income to their inhabitants. When the ferry goes, life whithers; cafes serve fewer coffees, guest houses make up fewer beds, seafarers look out to sea rather than back towards the land.

So far, so mournful, yet there is a fascinating counter-current: that of the almost inevitable 'save-our-ferry' campaign typically instigated by the local press in conjunction with the jilted port owner after the withdrawal of a lifeline link. Among the more resolute of these have been the long campaign during the 1990s to save Folkestone–Boulogne (ultimately unsuccessful) and efforts to see Newhaven–Dieppe endure (so far, so good). But undoubtedly the most plangent yet tenacious of these has been the recent campaign to resurrect the service between Swansea and Cork, which this year has seen the arrival of the co-operative-owned Fastnet Line and their cruise ferry *Julia*, the third attempt at creating an enduring connection between both Ireland and Wales' second cities.

Ever since the late 1970s, there has been something of a cloud over this service. With the new service now up and running during one of the most severe recessions seen in the Irish Republic in recent decades, we thought it would be appropriate to review the fascinating, campaigning history behind this well-known route.

THE INNISFALLEN WAY

The origins of the Cork service go way back to the Victorian era with the City of Cork Steam Packet operating a service between Ireland's second city and the Welsh port of Neyland on the River Cleddau. However as the 19th century drew to a close, construction began on a new deepwater port at Fishguard on the northern coast of Pembrokeshire. This opened in 1906 and the

City of Cork Steam Packet transferred their service to this state-of-the-art terminal, which at the time was using the steamships *Innisfallen* (built in 1896) and the *Inniscarra* (built in 1903). Sadly, neither ship survived the Great War, nor, really, did the City of Cork Steam Packet which, given the scale of its wartime losses, was obliged to be taken over by Coast Lines. Over the intervening decades, the Cork–Fishguard route was served by a variety of Coast Lines ships and it was not until the 1930s that the service saw significant transformation. This came at the start of the decade in the form of a newly constructed *Innisfallen*, a stately vessel, product of Harland & Wolff and the last of four similar vessels completed for the Coast Lines group at that time. Further change came mid decade with a re-organisation seeing the British & Irish name appear for the first time. The second *Innisfallen* lasted just a decade, being mined off Liverpool whilst deputising on that service in 1940.

As peace returned to Europe once again, B&I were quicker to resume normal service than they were a generation earlier. A new *Innisfallen* entered service in 1948 bringing new standards of size and luxury to the route and then in a blast from the past, in 1953 Coast Lines decided to resume the brand name City of Cork Steam Packet for the Fishguard service.

This state of affairs continued until the mid 1960s when Coast Lines sold the route to the Irish Government who resumed the name B&I. But the winds of change were blowing and the days of the traditional steamer service were numbered. With rakish British Rail ferries under construction and Viking invaders destined for the English Channel, it was time for B&I to enter the car ferry era.

THE CAR FERRY WAY

The close of the swinging sixties saw the greatest upheaval to the service to date with the eviction of B&I from Fishguard. This was undoubtedly something of a blessing in disguise as it forced the company to completely re-evaluate the future of the service as the era of the car ferry dawned. The company chose the Port of Swansea where a new ferry terminal was constructed in the River Tawe. The choice of port was far-sighted; Swansea was destined to be the western terminus of the new M4 motorway and would offer speedy vehicle access to the rest of southern Britain which the tortuous roads to Pembrokeshire never would.

And so in May 1969, the fourth *Innisfallen*, a remarkably modern-looking vessel with a spiky, futuristic funnel arrived at Swansea for the first time, opening the new route and enabling motorists to visit the South West of Ireland for the first time with comfort and convenience. She was fast, also, operating the service at almost 25 knots which would go some way to cope with the vagaries of the Welsh tides.

The car ferry *Innisfallen* was very much a ship of her generation: bold, dynamic and an exciting change from the elegant but terminally out-dated 'liners' of previous years. However, as was often the case in the early years of the modern car ferry era, her design was purchased from an existing template, that of Lion Ferry's trio of vessels constructed in the middle of the decade and commencing with the *Prins Bertil* in 1964. B&I signed for three: the 1968-built

The final **Innisfallen** is seen in the River Cleddau. She was built as the **Leinster** and moved to the Southern Corridor on the transfer of the Cork Connection to Pembroke Dock. (Miles Cowsill)

The **Fennia** was the final B&I-era car ferry on the Pembroke Dock-Cork service, closing the route in 1983. (Miles Cowsill)

The former **Innisfallen***, now named* **Ionian Sun** *is seen arriving at Swansea during her brief summer season in 1990. (Miles Cowsill)*

The **Celtic Pride** *is seen at Ringaskiddy shortly after her return to the route in 1991. (Miles Cowsill)*

Munster, and the1969-built *Innisfallen* and the *Leinster*. Swansea's *Innisfallen* and Liverpool's *Leinster* differed slightly from the other vessels in that they were eight metres longer and provided a rather more handsome profile.

The 1970s saw the route settle down into a comfortable pattern of overnight departures from Swansea and day returns from Cork. Traffic boomed, assisted by the entry into the European Community of both the UK and Ireland in 1973 and there was even talk of a second vessel to provide a true 'liner' service between the two ports with simultaneous departures from each terminal. However, both the port and the *Innisfallen* proved to have flaws: in the case of the former, the tide was an enduring issue with the timetable requiring significant flexibility. The *Innisfallen* was also somewhat lacking in cabins, a fact that was occasionally brought to the fore when relief cover was provided by the Scandinavian cruise ferry *Stena Germanica*.

So the closing years of the decade saw the order of a new, larger vessel for the service, the *Connacht*, constructed at Cork and earmarked to bring a significant increase in capacity and comfort to the Cork service. She was also earmarked for another significant development; the transfer of the service to a new port, some 60 miles further west at the former naval port of Pembroke Dock.

THE CLEDDAU WAY

B&I believed that 'economies' could be achieved through a shorter crossing from Pembroke Dock allowing more departures and reduced fuel consumption. There were also rumours that the *Connacht* was too large for Swansea, clearly untrue as she arrived there on her maiden voyage on 7th February 1979 and operated to the port for just over 100 days until the newly built terminal on the River Cleddau was opened. However, what soon became obvious was that Pembroke Dock was destined to become a new, southern hub for the company who were to open a proper short-sea route to Rosslare in County Wexford in 1980, taking the battle straight to Sealink and their historic Fishguard–Rosslare service. What also became very obvious was that the Cork route was doomed; the new, shorter, route to Cork had little advantage over the even quicker route to Rosslare.

These muddled decisions were exacerbated, if not potentially caused, by an emerging financial crisis at B&I which ultimately involved the removal of the *Connacht* and her replacement in autumn 1980 with the *Leinster*, the *Innisfallen*'s younger sister; clearly a retrograde step. Renamed *Innisfallen*, the ship operated to both Cork and Rosslare.

Prior to this fleet reshuffle, the first of what became a remarkable series of charter tonnage arrived at Cork in the form of the *Espresso Olbia*, originally Tor Line's *Tor Anglia*. She operated the service over the winter of 1979/80, beginning a trend which was to see a new vessel arrive at Pembroke Dock almost every year until the arrival of the *Isle of Inishmore* in 2001.

Meanwhile, at Cork, a new terminal was being constructed at Ringaskiddy that would reduce crossing times and avoid the passage up the River Lee. Ready for traffic by late 1982, B&I continued to sail to the older terminal upstream. Their bluff was called: if economies were required, the new terminal was vital; if the Cork route had a future, B&I would need to sign a contract for Ringaskiddy. This they were unwilling to do. Late in 1982, it was announced that the service would close in the New Year; in the event, it struggled on until 2nd February 1983 when the axe abruptly fell and sailings ceased.

However, the uncertainty was not over yet: the company soon announced that they would restore the Cork–Pembroke Dock route as a summer-only service from mid June to mid September and had acquired another charter vessel for the purpose. The superbly appointed Silja ferry *Fennia* took up the route for the duration of the summer and despite her clear superiority over any

previous vessel, the chaos and low credibility caused by the uncertainty of the previous year meant that the link was doomed. On 12th September 1983, the *Fennia* arrived at Pembroke Dock for the final time and the Cork Connection was no more.

THE CELTIC WAY

So began the wilderness years. Naturally enough, efforts immediately commenced to re-start the link; indeed they began before B&I had fully pulled out with a very short-lived freight service operating into Barry during spring 1983. However, it was not until 1984 that rumours emerged that Irish Continental Line were exploring the re-establishment of the route. Despite the fact that the company had recently restored the Liverpool–Belfast route previously dropped by P&O, the idea came to naught.

It seemed that the short-sea routes had triumphed and the *Innisfallen*'s way was gone for good. Just before Christmas 1986 came the news that the route was indeed to be revived, with four local authorities on either side of the Irish Sea having formed a consortium to operate the link, supported by local businessmen and led by Denis Murphy who became chairman of the new company. To be named Swansea Cork Ferries (SCF), the company had secured the time-charter of the former Silja cruise ferry *Aallotar*, latterly operating for Polferries as the *Rogalin*. As the *Celtic Pride* she would offer a nearly year-round service between the two cities and provide standards of service never previously seen on the Irish Sea. In an innovative move, the vessel would also be sub-chartered to Brittany Ferries to operate a mid-week Cork–Roscoff round trip.

After such a prolonged absence, the return of the ferry was greeted with nothing short of jubilation on both sides of the Irish Sea. Yet despite the celebrations, as the inauguration date approached, there were voices of dissent, particularly on the Welsh side. Prescient concerns were expressed about the Polish crew that would accompany the vessel during her tour of duty on the Irish Sea.

Regardless, on 15th April 1987, the Polish exile slipped away from Cork shortly after 21.00 and began her inaugural crossing to Swansea where she arrived at 07.20 the following morning. The wonderful, white, saviour ship had arrived, sailing in on a wave of enthusiasm. Plans were announced for a second freight-only vessel to arrive later in the year and businesses on both sides of the Irish Sea looked forward to times of plenty ahead.

Year one proved a success, with over 100,000 passengers being carried and the *Celtic Pride* was confirmed as returning to the service. Luxurious she may have been, however, her key weakness was that of a vanishingly small vehicle capacity. This led SCF to seek a replacement for the 1989 season and it was widely believed that Polferries' *Nieborow* would be the vessel in question.

However, as the 1989 season approached, it seemed that all was not well with the arrangements. Despite the success of the service, funding was required for the *Nieborow*, yet this was not forthcoming from the powers-that-were and so the option on both the *Celtic Pride* and the *Nieborow* passed. The Cork Connection was back to square one: no ferry, no service and very little hope. Had the celebrations of April 1987 evaporated so quickly?

As the new decade dawned, SCF were indeed sticking to their word and attempting to secure a charter to re-establish the service after its interregnum. In a remarkable turn of events, they announced the forthcoming arrival of Strintzis Lines' *Ionian Sun*, the former – and final – *Innisfallen*, making a return to her home port. Advertised as the 'Celtic Pride II' although never formally carrying that name, she operated a truncated five-month season but was not well liked by passengers.

So the following year, SCF returned to Poland and brought back the *Celtic*

The **Superferry**'s forward-facing Apollo lounge. (Miles Cowsill)

The **Superferry** lies over at Ringaskiddy whilst Brittany Ferries' **Val de Loire** loads for Roscoff. (Miles Cowsill)

*The **Superferry** is seen at her RIver Tawe berth during her first year on the Swansea-Cork service. (Miles Cowsill)*

*A smoky view of the **Superferry** arriving at Cork during her final years on the route. (Miles Cowsill)*

Pride. She re-opened the service in March 1991 and saw a further two years on the route. She departed for the final time in January 1993, a fine career somewhat marred by the tragic death of two teenagers on board in her final few months in service. As she left the route, it was clear that a fresh approach was needed as the local authorities could not maintain the focus required to run a modern ferry service. It was to the Greeks that the company turned once again and this time in a more dramatic way. SCF was to be sold to Strintzis Lines who were to transfer their *Superferry* to the Irish Sea as from April 1993.

The *Superferry* was a recent purchase by the Greek company and had just benefited from a comprehensive interior overhaul. The fact that a major European ferry operator was prepared to invest in the route, bringing one of their most modern vessels with them, was a massive vote of confidence. Indeed, such was the enthusiasm of the new owners, that they purchased the *Pegasus*, another former Silja ferry, to move to Swansea in 1994. Sadly, during her rebuild, she was destroyed by fire.

And so the *Superferry* settled into the familiar rhythm of the route. She was an idiosyncratic ship, never managing to quite shake off her Japanese origins yet providing a range of attractive facilities for the route. Whilst she was an appropriate choice for the post-*Celtic Pride* years, time soon caught up with her and as the 1990s drew to a close, it was to be hoped that a superior vessel would be sourced.

*Fastnet Line's **Julia** lies over at Ringaskiddy during April 2010. (Matthew Punter)*

Yet this was not something that Strintzis were able to fulfil and so in 1999, SCF was sold to its Irish management, by then led by Thomas Hunter McGowan. The *Superferry* was to be chartered for one last season, after which the company would look for a replacement. For 2001, the Hellenic Mediterranean vessel *Ville de Sete* was chartered and renamed *City of Cork*. She was another historic choice for the link, having previously served Cork–France as Irish Continental's *Saint Patrick II*. Never a long-term solution, she was replaced the following year by none other than the *Superferry* which was finally purchased by SCF. By now a rather tired ship, she returned to her old stomping grounds for a further six seasons until October 2006 when the plug was pulled: the ship was sold to the Red Sea and the route closed for the winter.

Having got rather a good price for their old workhorse, SCF were making very confident noises about returning in a blaze of glory in 2007. It was rumoured that they were close to acquiring the Fjord Line vessel *Atlantic Traveller* which would have been an ideal vessel for the route. Sadly, the sale fell through at the last minute and for 2007 there was to be no service.

*The bar area on the **Julia**. (Matthew Punter)*

The following year, SCF tried again: this time for the Color Line cruise ferry *Christian IV*, originally the 1981-built *Olau Britannia* and at the time one of the largest and most luxurious ferries in the world. Once again, events conspired against them. Her replacement was delayed from the shipyard and therefore the *Christian IV* needed to spend another few months on the Skagerrak, thus missing the start of the season. Could the Cork Connection sail once more? Swansea Cork Ferries, thwarted for two consecutive years, did not stick around to find out. Nothing was heard of the company again.

THE CO-OPERATIVE WAY

It was never an altogether sensible move to sell one's only ferry, operating a lifeline service, before a replacement was secure, a fact that the tourist industry in counties Cork and Kerry were all-to-acutely aware. After two failed seasons, the clamour for someone, anyone, to step into the breech became deafening. A campaign was formed in West Cork to put pressure on the authorities, anyone, to re-establish the link, but times were different, far tougher than they were in the 1980s.

By the start of 2009, it became obvious to the energetic bunch of local novices that if they wanted to see a ferry service return to the route, they were

*A dusk view of the **Julia**'s departure from Cork during May 2010. (Matthew Punter)*

The Fastnet a la carte restaurant on board the **Julia**. *(Matthew Punter)*

The **Julia***'s full-width bridge. (Matthew Punter)*

The **Julia** *is seen bow-in at Swansea in May 2010. (Matthew Punter)*

going to have to do it themselves. The West Cork Tourism Co-op (WCTC) was formed to spearhead the initiative and seek funds from local businesses and individuals on both sides of the Irish Sea. Within a matter of weeks, sufficient finances had been pledged for the co-operative to travel to Finland to bid for a vessel in open auction: this was none other than the former *Christian IV*, by then named *Julia* after an unsuccessful few months operating in the Gulf of Finland. Despite being initially unsuccessful at auction, after a protracted period of negotiation with the liquidators, the WCTC managed to secure the vessel. Disappointingly, this came too late for the 2009 season, leaving the tourist industry without a service for the third year running.

It was announced that the new service would commence in March 2010 being operated by Fastnet Line, a subsidiary of the WCTC. Although the co-operative had secured the *Julia* for a knock-down price, further fundraising was still needed for operating capital. Eventually, in late September, the vessel arrived at Cork where she spent the winter being certified and generally spruced up, whilst Fastnet established themselves as a ship-operating company.

The service had an impromptu maiden voyage on 10th March from Swansea, fresh after a protracted period of overhaul. Following a few electrical teething problems over the following week, the ship has since settled down into her routine, having benefited enormously during her initial months through the volcanic eruption in Iceland.

The *Julia* is certainly a welcome addition to the Southern Irish Sea, offering the most luxurious facilities yet seen between Cork and Swansea. Her sailing schedule is less ambitious than the SCF years, offering only four return crossings a week but of course, she has entered service whilst the economies of both the UK and Ireland are still under severe stress.

THE WAY AHEAD

Fastnet Line's arrival on the route has certainly been a remarkable story of perseverance and sheer willpower. Whilst the economic context is in many ways extremely challenging, there are also benefits. The driving force behind the re-establishment of the route has been the desire of local people to see their businesses in with a fighting chance of surviving the recession and the ferry service is in a very real way, a lifeline. Fastnet have looked to Brittany Ferries for inspiration: after all, this massively successful French firm began life as a farming co-operative in much the same way.

The Cork Connection is, for now, safe: providing operating costs can be covered, WCTC own their vessel and are intent on managing their route in the interests of the whole community. The long-term future, of course, depends on sufficient numbers of passengers and freight vehicles being carried to make what is undoubtedly a large vessel pay. The Fastnet chapter is the latest in this most interesting of sagas: that of two communities, divided by two hundred miles of sea, striving to maintain this tenuous link against all the odds. The Irish Government has tried; local authorities have endeavoured; private enterprise has attempted; even the Greeks have had a go.

It is now time for the People to see what they can do.

With thanks to Paul O'Brien of West Cork Tourism Co-op, Leslie Clarke (ABP) and Ivor Lewis (formerly ABP Swansea) for their assistance with this article.

7 Photo Feature - Guernsey by Sea
by Tony Rive

Over the years Guernsey has established itself as an important port of call for the variety of cruise ships serving Western Europe. With the deep and sheltered waters between Guernsey and Sark, vessels of all sizes are able to anchor in most weather conditions. Guernsey, like Jersey, has the advantage of not being a member of the European Union and is able to still offer visitors tax-free goods and duty-free sales.

In addition to the busy cruise ship theme, the services of Condor and the smaller ferry operators play an important integral part at St Peter Port. All the year round the *Commodore Clipper* and her operating partner the *Commodore Goodwill* are regular visitors to the port on most days. During the height of the summer season there is a variety of services to the adjoining islands and France.

Built by Koninklijke Scheldegroep B.V., Vlissingen, Holland in 1996 the ship entered service for Commodore Shipping in March 1996 on the Portsmouth-Guernsey-Jersey and St Malo service. The vessel is freight only with a capacity of 12 passengers, mainly lorry drivers. The ship is 126 metres long and has a gross tonnage of 11,166. The **Commodore Goodwill** was the second of two ships built in this class, the **Island Commodore** being the first which ran back to back on the Portsmouth-Channel Island service with the 'Goodwill'.

St Peter Port saw a busy afternoon on 26th July 2008. As with most days during the summer months, the port is bustling with private yachts and motor craft entering and exiting. Add a large cruise ship in the Russel, this time the **Grand Princess** with her tenders running back and forth to the ship, as well as passenger ships **Commodore Clipper** and the Manche Iles Express ferry **Victor Hugo** to the equation and it makes the port a great place to take photographs.

Sark Shipping runs three vessels to the small island of Sark which is situated 9 miles east of Guernsey. The island is approximately 3 miles by 1 mile and has a population of about 300 which swells during the summer months. Their passenger-only vessel is the **Bon Marin de Serk** which is Sark Shipping's oldest vessel. Built in 1983 by McTay Marine on the Wirral at Bromborough, the vessel carries 131 passengers and runs a daily service between Guernsey and Sark in the summer and a limited service during the winter months. The **Sark Venture** was built by Tees Inshore Engineering, Middlesbrough in 1986 and was chartered by Sark Shipping as the **Tie Venture II** in December 1990, after sea trials on the route in 1989. The vessel was used to carry freight to Sark before having a passenger cabin fitted to carry 122 passengers and some freight on the aft deck. The vessel was not bought outright but instead leased through another Guernsey business, Onesimus Dorey. The **Sark Viking** was specially built for Sark Shipping in 2008 and almost broke the Island of Sark's Bank before permission was finally given the go ahead. The vessel started being built by Artisans Construction at Aberleri Boatyard, Aberystwyth but after money problems at the yard and slow progress in building, the vessel was towed to Appledore Shipyard where she was completed and now handles all Sark's freight and carries 12 passengers.

This InCat craft was built in Tasmania in 1993 (hull 30) and was delivered to Condor Ferries to operate between Weymouth, Guernsey and Jersey in the summer of 1994. The 74-metre Wavepiercer was Condor's first car-carrying vessel. Since then she has operated between New Zealand's North and South Islands as **The Lynx** during the (northern) winters of 1994/95 and then during the (northern) summer of 1995 the vessel ran from Helsinki to Tallinn as the **Viking Express 1**. The **Condor 10** returned to the Channel Islands in 2002 and began the service linking Guernsey and Jersey with St Malo until June 2010 when it closed the service. She is now in Weymouth waiting to be sold, following the **Condor Rapide** being purchased in 2010.

With the demise of the **Condor 10**, the **Condor Rapide** joined Condor Ferries on 13th May 2010. Built by Incat, Hobart (hull 045), the craft was initially operated by the Australian Navy from 10th June 1999 and ran as HMAS **Jervis Bay.** The 86-metre ship was given Battle Honours whilst running troops between East Timor and Australia during the uprising between 1999 and 2000. The **Condor Rapide** carries 740 passengers, 180 vehicles and has a strengthened ramp to take lorries onto the vehicle deck.

*A product of the Fincantieri yard, the **Grand Princess** entered service in May 1998. The 108,806-ton ship looked majestic in the afternoon sunshine on 4th June 2010. The ship cost $450 million and is 290 metres long. Carrying over 3,000 passengers and crew, the ship is powered by twin diesel-electric motors of 42,000kW each.*

*Three ferries make up the fleet of vessels run by the French Company Manche Iles Express. The **Victor Hugo** (centre) was built in Norway in 1996 and named **Salten** before being bought by the present company. The vessel is an aluminium catamaran of 35 metres and has a service speed of 32 knots.. The **Marin Marie** (top) was built in Singapore in 1994 by Kvaerner Fjellstrand under the name of **Aremti**. The **Tocqueville** (foreground) was built in France (La Rochelle) in 2008. All three vessels ran services between Granville, Carteret and Dielette in France to Jersey/Sark/Guernsey and Alderney.*

*The **Herm Trident VI** is a steel hulled catamaran designed by Don Tate Associates of Lowestoft and was originally built at Gravesend in 1991. The vessel started life with a plywood superstructure but this was later rebuilt in aluminium after she was crushed and sunk by the **Norman Commodore** in St Peter Port on 14th June 1994 whilst moored at the end of the New Jetty. Marine and General Engineers repaired the vessel after she had been crushed.*

*This view takes in Celebrity Cruises' **Celebrity Century** and P&O Cruises' **Oceana**. The **Celebrity Century** was built in Germany at Papenburg and made her maiden voyage in 1995. P&O's **Oceana** was built at the Italian yard of Fincantieri as the **Ocean Princess**, originally for Princess Cruises. In 2002 she became the **Oceana** and was transferred to P&O Cruises to operate in the European market.*

A stern view of the **Arcadia***, which was originally destined for Holland America Line but prior to delivery was transferred to Cunard to become their new planned* **Queen Victoria***. Eventually prior to her completion she was transferred again within the Carnival Group to P&O Cruises to become their* **Arcadia***. The vessel is seen here anchored off St. Peter Port pending her evening departure to Southampton.*

The **Celebrity Eclipse** *and* **Celebrity Equinox** *both used Guernsey on 'shakedown' cruises before being named. The* **Celebrity Eclipse** *arrived off St Martin's Point in the early hours of 23rd April 2010 from Southampton. After clearing customs, the 122,000-ton ship headed straight to Bilbao to pick up stranded passengers stuck in Europe during the 'No Fly' period after the volcano erupted in Iceland. The 315-metre ship was built in Germany by Meyer Werft, at a cost of $641 million.*

*Another view of the **Bon Marin de Serk** leaving St. Peter Port outward bound for Sark. The services from Guernsey are an essential lifeline for residents of Sark as there is no all-year-round service operated from Jersey to the island. This vessel built in 1983 is able to accommodate 131 passengers and has cargo provision for stores and mail.*

*P&O Cruises' **Ventura** at the anchorage off St Martin's Point south of St Peter Port on 8th April 2008, with **Condor 10** inbound from St Malo. The **Ventura** was and still is one of the largest ships to visit Guernsey. At 116,000 tons the ship dwarfed the local pilot boat as she prepared to drop anchor. Built in Italy by Fincantieri, the vessel is 290 metres long with a 36-metre beam and a draft of 8.5 metres. She has 15 passenger decks and carries over 3,000 passengers.*

Fincantieri Built

by Brian D. Smith

The Italian shipbuilder Fincantieri can trace its routes back 200 years when the company was first recognised as a shipbuilding entity. Over the years it has built around 7,000 vessels and merged with various companies until in December 1959 a wholly new State Financial Holding Company was formed. Today it is the largest producer of luxury cruise ships anywhere in the world with an annual profit of around 58 million Euro on a turnover of over 2.46 billion Euro (September 2007). With its three main construction yards at Monfalcone, Venice and Genoa, the company has other yards in Ancona, Naples, La Spezia and Palermo where repairs and conversions are undertaken along with the construction of other ships such as luxury mega yachts, naval ships and other offshore vessels. With financial backing from the Italian Government, the company has also invested in yards across the world including the Lloyd Werft facility in Germany and several yards in the United States allowing the company to undertake work for the US Navy which otherwise would be precluded. The company also has several subsidiaries which specialise in their own particular field of shipbuilding and repair.

MAIN PLAYER

Today there are three main players in the European cruise ship construction industry. Fincantieri in Italy, STX Europe in Finland and France, and Meyer Werft in Germany. In recent times STX has achieved much public recognition with the construction of the world's largest cruise ship *Oasis of the Seas* for Royal Caribbean Cruise Lines while Meyer Werft have always generated large amounts of publicity for their clients with their newbuilds transiting the River Ems from their base in Papenburg to the North Sea. Fincantieri by comparison have remained almost anonymous but have continued building large numbers of cruise ships at their various yards to the great satisfaction of their customers. All three companies have invested heavily in cruise ship production and now newbuilds can be ordered and completed in less than two years. On average they turn out two or three cruise ships a year meaning that there is capacity to produce around one million tons of cruise ship per annum. With yards in the Far East, most notably the South Koreans, making strong representations about entering this very lucrative market, it is clear that the industry is entering an age where capacity outstrips demand.

In 2009 only Fincantieri managed to secure a new cruise ship order, a third unit of the 130,000-gross ton *Carnival Dream* class for Carnival Cruises. This went a long way to helping secure the jobs of Fincantieri's 9,000 employees (which rises to around 23,000 when you take into consideration subcontractors and suppliers). Things picked up a bit in 2010 when on 4th May Princess Cruises confirmed an ordered for two new prototype cruise ships, each to be around 141,000 gross tons. With a passenger capacity of 3,600 they will be the largest cruise ships built by Fincantieri. STX France have also

*The hull of Carnival Cruises' 130,000-gross ton **Carnival Magic** nears completion at the Monfalcone yard of Fincantieri in July 2010. She is the second of a three-ship order and is the largest ship ever built in Italy.*

The **Carnival Dream** is seen here during an early stage of construction. Note she has propellers and shafts rather than the more modern Amuzi pod propulsion found on most new cruise ships.

Steel for the new ships is cut by electronic laser. The procedure is carried out under water to stop the metal buckling under the extremely high temperatures generated during this process.

At the Monfalcone yard two new mobile cranes have a combined lifting capacity of 2,000 tons. They are on tyres rather than rails meaning they can go anywhere in the yard.

*The **Costa Fortuna** was completed in 2003 and is based on the parent company's **Carnival Destiny** class of ship. She is seen here leaving Venice in June 2009.*

*The **Costa Pacifica** was named at a joint celebration with the **Costa Liminosa** in Genoa earlier this year.*

*On 2nd July 2009 the keel for the new Cunard **Queen Elizabeth** is lowered into the building dock of the Monfalcone yard in front of Carol Marlow and other invited guests.*

In this stern view of the **Queen Elizabeth** *the base of the engine room is seen. The engines and generators were lifted in shortly after.*

secured two new large builds with the Italian Cruise Line MSC ordering another of their 137,000-gross ton *Fantasia* class vessels for delivery in 2012 and GNMTC (General National Maritime Transport Company) ordering a one-off 139,400-gross ton vessel. The combined tonnage of all cruise ships ordered since the downturn in 2008 is only 689,336 gross tons when there has been capacity in Europe alone to build over two million gross tons.

QUESTIONS

At the recent float-up ceremony of Oceania Cruises' new flagship *Marina*, their President Bob Binder said that pre-2008, a ship operator sat down with the prospective builders and asked them three questions: 1. When can you deliver? 2. What is the price? 3. How are we going to finance the newbuild? Today the situation is reversed and reads: 1. How are we going to finance the newbuild? 2. What is the price? 3. When can you deliver? It is no secret that the yards have been touting all major cruise lines for business with fantastic deals being offered for newbuilds. Prices, which had risen well above the rate of inflation for the last ten years, are suddenly dropping at substantial rates. One unofficial source told this writer that the price of a new ship is about 20% less than it was 24 months ago.

Shipbuilding by definition is a capital intensive, low margin industry process and Fincantieri has a particular difficulty in generating a higher return. Their youngest yard at Monfalcone is over 100 years old (Meyer Werft is only 35 years old) and like all their other yards are so linked to the social and industrial network of their respective locations that the company has found it too expensive to move. The location of the yards at the heart of industrial cities means it has been difficult to expand at a time when increasing vessel sizes demand larger building docks and longer outfitting piers. The Genoa yard is very site restricted by the town and by the local railway which passes right through the centre of the shipyard. The steel works are on one side of the railway whilst the building dock is on the other. Plans are being discussed to abandon the site north of the railway and to expand along the seafront. However, this is not without complications as the area has already been partially developed with a new marina and the city's airport. While Fincantieri sees its presence around Italy as a network of shipyards, it has led to duplication of

Opposite Page: Two months later and the superstructure is at an advanced state of construction. The ship was completed less than 15 months after the keel laying.

specialist equipment which the company seeks to harmonise. Fincantieri are currently investing in all of their yards to make them more suitable for the requirements of 21st century shipbuilding. Monfalcone has just taken delivery of one of the world's largest mobile cranes with a lifting capacity of 1,000 tons. This mammoth structure is on wheels rather than rails as in other yards which means that in theory it can lift large sections of ship and take them anywhere in the yard instead of just the dry dock. They have also streamlined their steel production and are making their modular production more efficient. In Castellamare, Fincantieri are still building ships on a slipway rather than a modern building dock which is labour intensive and far more expensive. They are in talks with the local authority about purchasing additional land so that a modern building dock can be constructed but with the current downturn it may never actually be built. The yard at Ancona has a modern dry dock but it does not have a fitting-out pier. For ordinary seagoing vessels that only require a month or two of outfitting this is not a problem but for modern cruise and passenger ships which can require up to six months of outfitting this is a major problem as work on the next project cannot start until the previous ship is fully completed.

OVER 60 CRUISE SHIPS

In the last 20 years Fincantieri has delivered over 60 cruise ships and is currently building vessels for Cunard, Carnival Cruise Line, Princess Cruises and for the luxury cruise lines Silversea's Cruises, Compagnie Du Ponant and Oceania Cruises (yes there is a recession on). If you look at most of Fincantieri's major orders you will see that with the exception of the luxury cruise brands most of their customers are under the Carnival Umbrella of Companies. Since 1990 this one company has ordered 49 cruise ships from Fincantieri. They have five more waiting to be delivered from the Italians and will probably order more later this year. The breakdown for the relative Carnival companies is as follows: Holland America Line 14 ships: P&O Cruises 3 ships: Costa Cruises 7 ships: Cunard Cruise Line 2 ships: Princess Cruises 13 ships while Carnival themselves have 10 ships with two currently under construction. When you consider that Carnival have also ordered 5 ships from Meyer Werft for their Aida Cruise line and 9 from STX for Princess Cruises and their own brand you can see why Fincantieri are so keen to remain as the ship yard of choice for the world's largest cruise company.

Without doubt their premier yard is the Monfalcone facility which, along with STX's yard in France are the only two yards in Europe that in theory have no limit on the size of ship that they could build. All ships from Finland are restricted in height by the Great Belt Bridge linking Denmark and Sweden and Meyer Werft by the width and depth constraints of the River Ems. The *Oasis of the Seas* project budgeted around £2 million to install a mechanical device which lowered the height of the funnel just for the delivery trip. Once it had passed under the Great Belt Bridge the funnel uptakes were raised back into position and the device disconnected forever! Any size ship can be built at Monfalcone and then delivered straight into the open sea.

The year 2010 has been a good year for Fincantieri with the group still confirming new orders and four luxury large cruise ships being delivered. In January the 92,000-gross ton *Queen Elizabeth* was floated up for the first time and construction commenced on the 130,000-gross ton *Carnival Magic*. The United Arab Emirates ordered two new naval vessels and the *Costa Deliziosa* was delivered to Costa Cruises. This 450 million Euro ship was the third cruise liner to be delivered by Fincantieri in nine months. The first of two luxury 69,000-gross ton cruise ships for the American company Oceania Cruises was launched at the Genoa yard on 26th February. Named *Marina* she is in the luxury mid-sized cruise ship bracket with only 1,200 passengers. Steel cutting for her sister

Oceania Cruises first newbuild **Marina** *is seen here with her stern section being welded to the superstructure. Note the rudder mounting on the starboard side.*

ship *Riviera* also started on the same day with invited guests attending both ceremonies. At the Ancona shipyard in April there was the launch of *L'Austral*, the first of two super luxury cruise ships ordered from Fincantieri by the French Owner Compagnie Du Ponant. Due to take up service in autumn 2010 the 10,700-gross ton ship is very similar to a mega yacht. The new ship, which will fly the French flag, is 142 metres long and 20 metres wide. Passenger capacity is only 260 and passengers will be accommodated in 132 cabins, all of which have a sea view or a private balcony. P&O Cruises' *Azura* was also delivered in April which brought to an end the Grand class ship design of which every unit was built at Monfalcone except the *Diamond Princess* and the *Sapphire Princess* which were built by Mitsubishi Heavy Industries in Korea. This was closely followed in July by the delivery of the *Nieuw Amsterdam* for Holland America Line and finally the *Queen Elizabeth* for Cunard in October. These last two ships are probably going to be the last of the versatile Vista class ships for Carnival-branded companies which have proved to be so successful. Not as large or as bulky as the Grand class design they are certainly more graceful, have better sea-keeping qualities and are capable of serving anywhere on the planet. A fact best demonstrated by both Cunard's Vista ships and P&O's sole representative undertaking world cruises every January.

AMERICAN BRANCH

The American branch of the company have also had a good 2010. In April Marinette Marine Corporation (Fincantieri's US subsidiary) and Boeing announced they are to team up to tender for the American Navy's Ship-to-Shore Connector program which provides for the construction of 80 new generation hovercraft. Marinette Marine will build the hulls while Boeing will build the propulsion, communication and control systems. The ten-year program provides for the construction of 80 hovercraft, for a total value of approximately $4 billion which will replace the Landing Craft Air Cushion

vehicles currently in service. In the same month Marinette Marine also won a $73 million contract from the National Oceanic and Atmospheric Administration for a Fisheries Survey Vessel and a $63 million contract for 30 newbuilds for the US Coast Guard. The research vessel is funded under the American Recovery and Reinvestment Act, a program to replace outdated vessels with new cutting edge ships. Construction of the vessel will be at Marinette shipyard in Wisconsin and delivery is scheduled for 2013 to the ship's home base in San Diego. The ship will serve the Southwest Fisheries Science Centre in southwest America, replacing the *David Starr Jordan* which has logged over 1.5 million miles since entering service in 1966. At 63.5 metres long and with a 15.2-metre beam, the vessel will be equipped with ultra modern instrumentation for sampling and advanced navigation systems with multi-frequency acoustic sensors and extensive laboratories. The vessels for the US Coast Guard will be built at Green Bay, Wisconsin, and are part of a multi-year Coast Guard program at a total contract value of $600 million. Delivery of the first vessel is scheduled for late 2011. This order brings the number of vessels built in America by Fincantieri to 97.

With both Meyer Werft and STX Finland yet to confirm any new cruise ship orders since the downturn in 2008, Fincantieri have demonstrated that they have the capability and confidence to survive and diversify in these difficult times. Although with major discounting now being offered by all three yards the only real obstacle to new ships being ordered is the reluctance of the major financial institutions to fund newbuilds. As the credit crunch starts to ease, and there are signs that it is starting to do so, new cruise ships will start to fill the order books of the main players. Without doubt Fincantieri will continue to build large luxury cruise ships for some time. By diversifying into less lucrative but more stable markets and investing in other countries, the company should be flying the Italian flag for shipbuilding for some time yet.

*View taken from the mast of the **Marina** showing an overview of Fincantieri's Genoa yard.*

*In April 2010 the **Marina** is ready for floating up. She went for sea trials in September 2010 and will be handed over to her owners in January 2011. A sister ship **Riviera** will follow in 2012.*

9 The Life and Times of the Kungsholm
by Ann Haynes

They say beauty is in the eye of the beholder, and on a spring day in March 1966 in Gothenburg, Sweden, the huge crowds welcoming the newest ship in the Swedish American Line fleet must have thought they were looking at perfection when the white-hulled *Kungsholm* sailed into the harbour with the distinctive three golden crowns logo on each of her two funnels. She was the latest vessel to be designed and built for the Line, and her design trajectory can be traced back to the latter 1930s.

SWEDISH AMERICAN LINE

Swedish American Line (SAL) – a subsidiary of Brostrom AB, the famous Gothenburg ship owners and industrialists – was formed in late 1914 but it was not until well after the end of the Great War that the line was able to provide a mainly emigrant service from Gothenburg to New York with the previously owned ships *Stockholm* and *Drottningholm*. As the flow of emigrants slowed in the early 1920s, the company decided to take advantage of the North American trade to Scandinavia and placed an order with Armstrong, Whitworth on the Tyne in the United Kingdom, for a two-funnelled, diesel-driven passenger ship of 18,815 tons. In 1925 the *Gripsholm* came into service for tourist and business passengers and was so successful that the company promptly ordered a further vessel.

This time the order was placed with Blohm & Voss, Hamburg, and so in 1928 the first *Kungsholm* to be designed and built specifically for Swedish American Line took to the seas at 21,250 tons. This was another diesel motor ship, with two tall raked funnels and masts, an attractive counter-stern and wonderful furnishings and decorations for both first and tourist class accommodation. These features, styled by the Swedish architect and designer Carl Bergsten, were designed to appeal to the American market and did this most successfully. The ship sailed between Gothenburg and New York as a trans-Atlantic liner, with occasional cruises, and indeed her fame was marked by the writing of 'The Kungsholm Song' in the 1930s; this was recorded by SAL Chief Purser Evert G. Eriksson who became known as 'The Singing Purser', and was sung at many a Farewell Dinner on the ship.

The Company next planned another cruise ship, which was to be the 1941 *Stockholm*, designed largely by their Naval Architect Erik Christiansson, but the triple-screw motor ship suffered a fire during construction. She was repaired and completed with a larger superstructure than first intended but this led to stability problems. She was a three-class ship, designed for the trans-Atlantic run and one-class cruising like her forbears but with air-conditioning. She was delivered late, so the Second World War put paid to her use by the neutral-throughout Swedish American Line, leaving her in the builder's yard to be sold to the Italian Line for use as a troopship, before bombing caused her to capsize in Trieste harbour. The Second World War also saw the sale of the 1928 *Kungsholm* to the Americans for use as a troopship, thus ending her career with SAL.

After the war, the Company ordered another smaller *Stockholm*, for delivery in 1948. This was a passenger/cargo liner, sailing between Gothenburg, Copenhagen and New York. She became notorious worldwide

Swedish American Line contracted with shipbuilders John Brown & Company (Clydebank) Ltd. for their new **Kungsholm** and work began in January 1965. She was named by the Swedish American Line Chairman's wife Mrs Annabella Brostrom on 14th April 1965. (Mick Lindsay collection)

when, in dense fog in July 1956 off the American coast, she rammed the Italian Line ship *Andrea Doria*, which sank with the loss of 52 lives.

Next, the Company ordered a third *Kungsholm* to be built in Vlissingen (Flushing) at 21,165 tons and in 1953 this fine two-funnelled diesel-engined vessel took to the seas for liner service and cruising. The naval architects had wanted a modern-looking ship with only one funnel but the Company decided otherwise and so the forward one had to be a dummy, albeit slightly taller than the other. Furnishings and decoration were of the highest quality and best design, well suited to this elegant ship before she was sold in 1965 after years of sailing between Gothenburg and New York. SAL had a policy of maintaining a young fleet, selling tonnage relatively quickly to help finance newbuildings with the latest refinements.

In 1954 a new *Gripsholm* was ordered and in 1957 the 23,190-ton Italian-built ship began her cruising career. Sailing trans-Atlantic she was a two-class ship but became one-class when cruising. With many rooms designed by the

*The beautiful new **Kungsholm** with her Swedish American Line colours of white hull and superstructure, and two masts, is pictured at Southampton. Her two funnels each bear the Company logo of three golden crowns, set within a blue circle, on each side. (Bruce Peter collection)*

*Despite being a huge success, the **Kungsholm** was sold by Swedish American Line and operated out of New York from October 1975 for Norwegian-owned Flagship Cruises. The only outward change they made was to feature their own logo on the funnels. (Bruce Peter collection)*

Italian architect Nino Zincada, the ship was thought to be even more elegant than her predecessors, and passengers chose to travel on her for her particularly luxurious style, similar to other Italian-designed ships of the period, and offering reputedly perfect service on board.

So with all these stylish and well-crafted ships as antecedents, a new *Kungsholm* was planned by the Company, as a running mate for the *Gripsholm*. She was to be capable of the Gothenburg to New York run, but for most of her time was to be used as a cruise ship.

A NEW *KUNGSHOLM*

In December 1962 John Brown & Company (Clydebank) Limited wrote to Swedish American Line in Gothenburg asking to tender for the new ship and after much negotiating between both companies, it was agreed that John Brown would do so by the deadline of 4th June 1963. John Brown at this time was hoping to build the proposed new Cunard liner, known then as 'Q3', but the planning of the vessel had dragged on since the early 1960s and the shipyard was worried that it would not be able to retain its craftsmen, particularly those who outfitted liner interiors. These were the key workmen and absolutely vital to the success of the company and its shipbuilding future. It was these skilled people who were needed to continue the shipyard's reputation for building spectacular vessels such as the *Queen Mary*, *Queen Elizabeth*, HMS *Vanguard* and the Royal Yacht *Britannia*.

Here I must mention another ship that is dear to my heart: the *Transvaal Castle* of 1961. This was the 'Hotel Class' Mail Ship of the famous Union-Castle Line, on which I worked as a Purserette when I first went to sea with the line in late 1965. Once the *Transvaal Castle* had left the yard, other work had to be found and that is why John Brown's had written to Swedish American Line about their proposed new ship. Their tightly budgeted tender proved successful at £6,780,000 with a delivery date of October 1965, and this seems to have been the start of John Brown's troubles.

Under Yard Number 728, construction on *Kungsholm* began in the shipyard in January 1965. She was to be similar to previous ships of the Swedish American Line with two funnels and two masts, and most of her time would be spent cruising; the interior decorations would be of the finest, and beautifully designed and crafted for the expected 450 passengers. For her infrequent Atlantic passages, she would carry 108 Cabin Class passengers and 605 in Tourist Class.

The propulsion was to be twin-screw nine-cylinder 25,200 bhp diesel engines, which were built by AB Gotaverken of Gothenburg, Sweden. Their design brief was engines to achieve a service speed of 21 knots, faster than anything achieved by former SAL ships, and in fact when built she was the most powerful motor ship in the world.

It would appear that the yard took on the order simply to keep their skilled workers in jobs, so the price took no account of wage inflation, industrial unrest and changes in the outside economy. The inevitable happened and the delivery date had to be renegotiated and changed to December 1965 which resulted in the shipyard having to pay financial penalties for the late delivery, said to be £3 million.

Swedish American Line had specified that the ship was to be of 26,670 gross tons, with a length of 660 feet, breadth of 87 feet, and draught of 28 feet. Detailed research had been done both in Gothenburg and also in the SAL New York offices and so they expected the utmost care in the design and construction which was overseen by the naval architect Claes Feder. Born in Madeira to a Danish father and Swedish mother, after the Second World War he went to Scandinavia and studied Naval Design and Engineering at Gothenburg University before qualifying and starting his career. During this

The comfortable and spacious Forward Lounge on the **Kungsholm***'s Promenade Deck, and just below the Bridge, was partly designed by Count Sigvard Bernadotte. It had wonderful forward-facing views, a rosewood dance floor and a long bar. (Burkhard Schütt collection)*

The Main Lounge on the **Kungsholm***'s Verandah Deck, which extended the full width of the ship, under a coved ceiling, was probably the most impressive space on the ship. It contained many contemporary art works - including the Midnight Sun ceramic bas-relief and sliding decorative panels - amidst the luxurious surroundings. (Burkhard Schütt collection)*

The Aft Library on the **Kungsholm** *was on Verandah Deck, on the port side; the comfortable furnishings and writing desks in this yew-panelled room provided a delightful place for relaxation. (Burkhard Schütt collection)*

The Forward Cocktail Lounge on Verandah Deck port side was yet another luxurious and well-designed location. With its wood-panelled bar, art work and views of the sea, it proved very popular with passengers. (Burkhard Schütt collection)

For the athletically inclined (as the brochure called them), there was an Indoor Swimming Pool available, with comfortable seating around it for those not inclined to swim. (Burkhard Schütt collection)

The Lido Deck and its sheltered Swimming Pool were very popular on the **Kungsholm**. In the background can be seen the forward funnel, which was actually a dummy, containing generators and water tanks. However, the two funnels helped create the most balanced and beautiful ship design. (Burkhard Schütt collection)

time he worked for a while as a Purser on the *Stockholm* plying between Gothenburg and New York and, coincidentally, he met a Swedish passenger on board and subsequently married her. After many years as a successful naval architect, he was chosen to be Chief Designer for the new vessel, and this was to be one of the highlights of his early career.

The comfortable and spacious Promenade Deck Forward Lounge, with a nod to American tastes for anything Royal, was partly designed by Count Sigvard Bernadotte. He was one of the Swedish Royal Princes who had lost his title by marrying a commoner but who was a distinguished industrial designer in his own right; the Lounge had wonderful forward-facing views, a dance floor and long bar; aft of this between the funnels was a lido buffet area. On the Verandah Deck below was the auditorium designed by British architect Geoffrey Tabb, used as cinema, theatre, lecture hall and church; to one side of this was the yew-panelled library. The ship's main Lounge, which extended the full width of the ship, was by the interior designer Robert Tillberg, and was the most impressive space on the ship, with its coved ceiling and comfortable seating for 450 people. Three decks below this on A Deck was the beautiful full-width Dining Room, which could be partitioned for two-class Atlantic service and passengers were told they would experience the ultimate in luxury on a ship designed for luxury.

On 14th April 1965 the ship was launched and named *Kungsholm* by Mrs Annabella Brostrom, the wife of the Swedish American Line Chairman and in late 1965 the vessel completed her successful sea trials on the Clyde. In January 1966 'The New York Times' as usual reported the daily arrival and departure of ships into the port, but added that the maiden arrival and cruise voyage of SAL's new ship had been postponed as a result of a delayed delivery by the shipbuilder. They also mentioned that the *Kungsholm* was being built at Clydebank, in a pier adjacent to the new *Queen Elizabeth 2*, and was a gleaming passenger ship teeming with welders. It seems obvious that the port of New York was eagerly awaiting the new ship, on her first sailing from her home port of Gothenburg. Back on the Clyde, with her fitting out complete, on 17th March 1966 she was handed over to Swedish American Line and sailed to Gothenburg ready for the Swedish-designed furniture and furnishings to be put on board.

INTO SERVICE

The *Kungsholm* sailed on her maiden voyage from Gothenburg on 24th April 1966 with 304 passengers, under her Captain Per Eric Sjolin, and experienced all kinds of weather on her trans-Atlantic crossing. The 'New York Times' described her arrival on 2nd May 1966 with great excitement: she arrived with a bang, they said, explaining that a 340-year-old bronze 24-pound gun, recovered from the Swedish ship *Vasa* in 1628, was fired four times from Battery Park in greeting and was answered by four blasts of the whistle/horn on board the beautiful *Kungsholm*. The ship had Swedish Kokum Super Tyfon horns, tuned to C-Natural and D-Sharp. Most of the great liners of the 1960s used this type of horn, in which the narrow end of the bell turns 90 degrees from the horizontal, so that condensed moisture would run down out of the power chamber and not cause corrosion to either the power chamber or the vibrating diaphragms.

There were fireboat water salutes and noisy greetings from all around her as she sailed into port after her maiden voyage, with the liner *United States* alongside an adjacent pier. Two successful charity events were held on the ship before she set off on her next voyage, and would-be passengers enjoyed the sight of a model of the ship in SAL's New York office window on Fifth Avenue.

The success of the maiden trans-Atlantic crossing continued with her

*This is a port side view of the **Kungsholm** when she was sailing for Flagship Cruises. She operated out of New York for them from October 1975. (Bruce Peter collection)*

*In 1978 Flagship Cruises sold the **Kungsholm** to P&O. She went to Bremen for 'modernising' which included removing one funnel and the main mast, and installing new cabins. Totally transformed, with one re-modelled funnel, in January 1979 she set off for Australia as the **Sea Princess**. (Trevor Jones)*

cruising itineraries, and one of these was a Spring Festival Excursion from New York to Finland in May 1967. After arriving in Stockholm, passengers could board the *Birger Jarl* and sail on her to Helsinki. The *Kungsholm*'s success was of course due to the ship and the impeccable service offered on board by her Swedish Officers and Crew.

In 1975, however, the Line toyed with the idea of registering the ship under a flag of convenience and this was reluctantly accepted by the stupefied New York office-staff, who had many forward bookings, and Swedish on-board staff. With full employment in Sweden in the 1970s, high wage rates made it hard to recruit and retain seafarers but unfortunately the Swedish unions would not accept the situation, believing that this would mean a change of crew nationality. Swedish American Line therefore made the astonishing decision to close their shipping business and sell the *Kungsholm*.

NEW OWNERS

Then the ship indeed became registered under a flag of convenience (Liberia), but for her new owners: the Norwegian Per and Oivind Lorentzen's company called Flagship Cruises Ltd, operating out of New York from October 1975, with only the funnel logo being changed. The brochures of the day waxed lyrical about the pleasures of cruising with 'The *Kungsholm* Touch'!

Flagship Cruises had sold two of their previous ships – the *Sea Venture* and *Island Venture* – to P&O Princess Cruises and so in 1978 it came as no surprise when they were persuaded to sell the *Kungsholm* to P&O as well, as a replacement for their *Arcadia*. The ship left New York for England with a small crew on board, who were ordered to throw china and everything loose

overboard (only Flagship Cruises' items by this time), as the new owners did not want them.

P&O registered the ship under the British flag and in November 1978 sent her to Bremen in Germany for 'modernising' work to match the style of their existing single-funnelled *Spirit of London*. More cabins with portholes were built into the Promenade Decks aft, breaking the window line. The main mast was removed, the forward funnel was cut down and the aft one heightened and remodelled into a rather weird 'cone' shape, thus transforming forever the look of this once-beautiful ship. She set off in January 1979 as the *Sea Princess* to cruise in Australian waters from Sydney, until 1981 when she returned to British cruising and also featured in a very popular American television series as the first 'Love Boat'. In 1982 P&O increased her passenger capacity to 840, and she sailed as part of the Princess Cruises fleet on the American west coast until 1991 when she returned to sail out of Southampton.

The *Sea Princess* changed name to *Victoria* in April 1995 to avoid confusion with the growing Princess Cruises fleet, and continued to work her traditional magic on her passengers. I count myself amongst that number as I cruised on her in 1998 in the Mediterranean.

By that time, I was one of the Directors of the re-launched Union-Castle Line, and part of the team involved in the planning of the Union-Castle Centenary Voyage, to celebrate in 1999/2000 the centenary of the amalgamation of Union Line and Castle Packets in 1900. This planning had been going on for several years amongst us, a small group of South of England business people who loved Union-Castle Line and their ships. A wonderful itinerary sailing around Africa, calling at ports historically linked

*The **Sea Princess** is seen in Cape Town, South Africa. (Trevor Jones)*

In 1982 the **Sea Princess** *had her passenger capacity increased to 840 by P&O before being sent to the American west coast Princess Cruises fleet. Here she is in dry-dock in Southampton in 1982. (Mick Lindsay)*

SEA PRINCESS
LONDON

with the Company, had been planned by my husband David, another Director of the re-launched Company, and himself a former Union-Castle Line Deck Officer who came ashore in 1967 to continue working for the Line in their London offices. A Business Report was written and financial backing was sought and duly found. The search for a suitable ship ended with the *Victoria* being chartered from P&O for the 66-night voyage, and I was so proud to sign the Charter Party document on behalf of Union-Castle Line. Despite the death of my beloved husband during this time, dear readers, we made it happen!

The *Victoria*'s funnel was painted in the distinctive vermilion red with black topping, and the whole ship, with Captain, Officers and Crew, became a Union-Castle vessel from 11th December 1999 when we set sail from Southampton. This famous ship and itinerary proved extremely popular with all the passengers, as we expected. They enjoyed the Carib Lounge, Lido Bar, Pool, Lido Buffet and Starlight Lounge on Lido Deck, and the International Lounge, Riviera Bar, Library, Shop and Theatre on Riviera Deck, as well as the elegant Coral Dining Room. Special festivities and items of memorabilia or ephemera to see or buy were also arranged and I was pleased to be able to arrange for the issue of a Commemorative stamp and First Day Cover by the St Helena Post Office to celebrate our call at St Helena in the South Atlantic. I was on board for the whole Centenary Voyage, partly as a passenger and partly as liaison between the Captain and my colleagues back at the Southampton office. It was emotionally and physically exhausting but everyone involved in the Union-Castle Line Centenary Voyage felt such a tremendous sense of achievement when we arrived back in Southampton on

15th February 2000.

The *Victoria* continued in P&O's service until sold in 2002 to Leonardo Shipping Inc. (Bahamas-registered); the sale was arranged by Kyma Ship Management Inc. whose current Chairman, since 1998, is Captain Paris Katsoufis. In 1997/98 Captain Katsoufis was President of Cunard Cruise Lines and relocated the company from New York to Miami, as well as positioning the company for sale to Carnival Corporation. The Kyma Ship group includes Leonardo Shipping, Topaz International Shipping (they owned *The Topaz*, the ex *Empress of Britain*) and Galini Enterprises. I like the thought that Leonardo Shipping's newest purchase was renamed *Mona Lisa*!

MONA LISA

On 22nd October 2002 I was one of the crowd watching the ship leave her home port of Southampton for the last time. Her passengers disembarked in Civitavecchia, Italy, on 2nd November, before the ship underwent yet another conversion, this time for her charter to German travel agents Holiday Kreuzfahrten, sailing as the *Mona Lisa*. The famous picture (by Leonardo da Vinci) was featured on both sides of the funnel, providing what some consider an eerie look to the ship. The ship sailed on (with one unfortunate temporary grounding on 25th July 2003 leaving the Magdalenenfjord, and another in Venice on 12th May 2004) until in September 2006 Holiday Kreuzfahrten declared insolvency, and she was sent to Piraeus by her owners.

She was then used as an accommodation ship for the 2006 Asian Games in Doha, Qatar, for two months, and this was to be followed by two eight-month charters as *The Scholar Ship*, a university at sea backed by Royal

*The **Sea Princess** had a name change to become the **Victoria** in April 1995, to avoid confusion with the growing Princess Cruises fleet. With a white hull and mast, and P&O yellow 'funnel', she gleams in the Southampton sunlight. (Bruce Peter collection)*

*With many passengers lining the rails on the open decks, P&O's **Victoria** sails on a calm sea, with her hull beautifully reflected in the blue water. (FotoFlite)*

The **Victoria** was chartered by the re-launched Union-Castle Line for a 66-day Centenary Voyage around Africa. She sailed from Southampton on 11th December 1999 with the distinctive vermilion red/black funnel and Union-Castle Line flags flying. (Mick Lindsay)

In 2002 the **Victoria** was sold to Kyma Ship Group, who chartered her out to German travel agents Holiday Kreuzfahrten. With a new name, **Mona Lisa** she sailed with them under charter until they declared insolvency in September 2006. Here she is in the Tagus off Lisbon in May 2003. (Bruce Peter)

Caribbean Cruise Line. It was planned that she would sail with Pullmantur Cruises after these first charters but first she went on a very short charter to Louis Cruise Lines as the *Oceanic II* in May 2007 after their loss of *Sea Diamond*.

She was then able to take up her charter with the Spanish Pullmantur Cruises, still as the *Oceanic II*, which is how she unexpectedly appeared in my life again when I was in Istanbul cruising on board the *Perla* in July 2007. What a delightful sight to see her berthed astern!

The ship's next summer cruises started in May 2008, during which time she became stuck on a sand bank on 4th May in the Irben Strait (Riga/Latvia). These cruises were with the German travel agents Lord Nelson Seereisen, who had exclusivity for bookings on her, sailing out of Bremerhaven under the name *Mona Lisa*. Instead of being laid up in the winter, she was chartered temporarily to the Peace Boat organisation to replace the then mechanically challenged *Clipper Pacific* (ex *Song of Norway*).

The *Mona Lisa* appeared in my life again on 25th August 2009 when I sailed on her out of Bremerhaven with the unexpected sound of Nat King Cole singing 'Mona Lisa, Mona Lisa' ringing in my ears. A seven-day cruise to ports between Bremerhaven and Cowes, Isle of Wight, had been booked with Lord Nelson Seereisen, so a congenial group of us enjoyed what we felt might be our last chance to see and sail on this ship. She certainly looked quite worn in places since I last sailed on her for the Union-Castle Line Centenary Voyage but it was a wonderfully emotional and enjoyable time on board.

On 11th September 2009 I was sailing with a group from the Ocean Liner Society on the *Aquamarine* out of Piraeus, Greece, and to my amazement when I looked across the azure sea I could see the white-hulled *Mona Lisa* heading towards and past us towards the shipyards of Perama. That was my

last sight of her in her natural element – the sea.

After some conversion work she sailed off to British Columbia, Canada, under a 56-day charter from Leonardo Shipping, as accommodation for the 2010 Vancouver Winter Olympic and Paralympic Games' workers at Squamish Terminals. She left in March 2010 for Kiel, Germany, to resume her cruises with Lord Nelson Seereisen and was the first cruise ship of the year to call at Kiel on 27th March. On 1st May she started her ten summer cruises, which were scheduled to continue until she returned from Greenland on 31st August 2010.

This historic and memorable ship contains large amounts of wood and veneers and I fear that, under the conditions of the SOLAS (Safety Of Life At Sea) regulations which came into force on 1st October 2010, her future may not be as long-lasting as we would hope, especially as it is known that scrap buyers have been looking at her details. A Swedish entrepreneur had been trying for five years to buy the ship if he could get permission to convert her into a floating hotel in Gothenburg; he was finally offered simply a five-year berth, so he withdrew his offer. His suggestion that the ship be used for student accommodation in Stockholm, with the possibility of this leading to a permanent mooring, has come to nothing. At the time of writing the ship is en route to Oman from Piraeus to become an accommodation ship. We can bear in mind that the 1959-built *Rotterdam* is enjoying a new lease of life as an hotel in Rotterdam, but one must also be realistic and remember that ships have a finite life.

Since being built in 1966 as the *Kungsholm* she has had a long, varied and fascinating career and I personally have so many memories of this wonderful ship. Long may the *Kungsholm* sail in whatever guise the future holds for her, even if it is only in our hearts and minds.

The **Mona Lisa**'s charter in May 2008 was with German travel agents Lord Nelson Seereisen, sailing out of Bremerhaven. Here she is in August 2009, temporarily anchored off the south coast of England near the Isle of Wight. (Mick Lindsay)

10 Ferries to Morocco
by Matthew Murtland

Sitting on the north-western edge of the African continent, Morocco is a vast and diverse country, approximately twice the size of the United Kingdom in area but with half the population. Much of the country is desert or mountainous and a majority of the populace lives towards the north where the great cities of Casablanca, Rabat, Fes and Tangier are found. Before gaining independence in 1956, most of Morocco was a protectorate of France and the French influence remains – particularly in trade and some aspects of culture, and as a language for commerce and trade. The connection is more tangibly seen in the migration of people: whilst there is now only a modest permanent population of Europeans in Morocco, since independence hundreds of thousands of Moroccans have settled in Europe, particularly in France whose Moroccan community is estimated to be in excess of a million.

At the peak of summer, when many of those European-based Moroccans return 'home' for extended breaks, more ferries operate from the north Moroccan coast to EU countries than between the UK and France. Unlike on the English Channel, however, the trade is more severely seasonal and much less freight-oriented. And, where years of development and investment have made crossing the Channel efficient and unremarkable, sailings to Morocco remain somewhat unpredictable, occasionally chaotic – but most definitely memorable.

SPANISH ENCLAVES

It is important to clarify the seemingly innocuous use of the term 'Morocco' which hides some important political nuances: in much the same way that Britain retains control of the Southern Spanish enclave of Gibraltar, Spain in turn has possessions of her own – fiercely disputed by Morocco – along the north African coastline, particularly Ceuta, 30 miles to the east of Tangier, and Melilla, just a mile across the bay from Morocco's primary Eastern port, Nador. Services to the enclaves are covered by a Spanish Government contract presently held by Trasmediterranea.

The juxtaposition of Nador and Melilla gives something of an insight into the cultural differences one finds aboard the ships themselves. Although in recent years the authorities have made attempts to keep the Moroccan ports clear of the touts and helpful 'guides' who hassle and sometimes distress sensitive European tourists, once outside the port complex things remain much as before – particularly in Nador where the 900 yards from the port to the Melilla border crossing can be a quite chaotic walk at the best of times. A concerted attempt by would-be immigrants to storm the border in 2005 led to six deaths and it is not uncommon to see baton-wielding policemen straining to keep control. Once into Melilla, with its sandy beach, bars and restaurants, the crowds on the Moroccan side suddenly seem a million miles away.

Acciona Trasmediterranea's 1999-built 92 metre InCat **Alboran** *is seen leaving Algeciras for Ceuta. (Matthew Murtland)*

COMANAV's **Al Mansour** (ex-**Reine Astrid**) pulls away from her berth in the Spanish port of Algeciras ahead of another crossing to Tangier. (Matthew Murtland)

The **Berkane** of COMARIT, originally SNCM's **Napoleon**, emits a spectacular plume of smoke from her funnel as she leaves Genoa for Tangier in July 2010. (Matthew Murtland)

Aboard the ships, things tend to be a little calmer – although the sight of young would-be stowaways attempting to shinny up your vessel's ropes for a free passage to Spain, their worldly possessions tied up in a plastic bag around their waist, is an occasional sobering pre-departure spectacle (albeit rarely successful). Almost universally, on routes other than to the Spanish enclaves, a mosque is provided aboard, sometimes in incongruous places: aboard the one-time *St Christopher* (now the *Ibn Batouta*), this was initially in the old 'Video Warp'; on *Le Rif* (ex-*Galloway Princess*), the Tom & Jerry Children's Play Area; and on the *Captain Zaman II* (ex-*Svea*, chartered by COMANAV in 2002) in the former casino.

CULTURAL DIFFERENCES

Without wishing to stereotype, there remain quite distinct social differences between 'European' and 'Moroccan' passengers. On the longer routes it is not uncommon to see the ageing cars and camper vans of returning Moroccans on the quayside many hours before departure, each vehicle crammed with baggage and often with electrical goods and furniture strapped to the roof. Perhaps not surprisingly, whereas Europeans tend to have cabins and gravitate to the bars and restaurants, Moroccan passengers more often travel in the reclining seat lounges, or 'camp out' in foyers and corridors – in some cases there are visible burn marks in the carpets where attempts have been made to cook using camp stoves! It is clear that the ships are given fairly unforgiving treatment: few things seem to be beyond pilferage, from toilet rolls (on longer crossings one is well-advised to bring one's own) and decorative features such as cabin corridor artwork through to fixtures and fittings. Sailing on the dilapidated *Oujda* (ex *Pride of Hampshire*, chartered by COMANAV) in 2006, our cabin had been robbed of its curtains, bunk bed ladder, the armrests and back to the chair and one of the life vests. Crew on the *Giulia d'Abundo* (ex *Quiberon*, briefly chartered by Euroferrys) advised that there had been a determined effort to remove the large television screens from the ship's two cinemas. On the *Wisteria* (ex *Duc de Normandie*), cabin passengers must ask at reception for towels where a sign advises that a deposit must be left – a policy often quite openly applied only to Moroccan passengers.

Whilst Nador is more of a transit port, Tangier to the west is a tourist destination in its own right. Before independence Tangier was an international zone under joint French, Spanish and British control and became famous as an exotic but cosmopolitan city. In the early 1970s it was even possible to sail direct from the UK on Southern Ferries' *Eagle* but, more recently, the widespread use of fast ferries has seen a dramatic shift in the nature of traffic. As recently as May 2003, well outside the peak season, I experienced the most incredible crush to board *Le Rif*, with Moroccan ladies fighting to be first aboard (and the right to first pick of the seats). Today, for much of the year the conventional ferries seem to be largely deserted, with passengers now loyal instead to the fast ferries. The transfer in the past year of most ferry traffic to the new industrial port of 'Tangier Med', 25 miles to the east of Tangier itself, has further removed a little of the magic of arriving in the bustling old port where, for now, some of the fast ferries continue to sail – beneath the heights of the Medina and the famous Hotel Continental, a favourite of Winston Churchill.

AN HISTORICAL PERSPECTIVE

For decades, crossings to Morocco were dominated by legacy French and Spanish operators, such as the Compania Trasmediterranea or the Compagnie Generale Transatlantique, providing classic liner or packet services. Trasmediterranea pioneered car ferry operations to the area in the early 1950s when their groundbreaking pair the *Victoria* and *Virgen de Africa* were introduced from Algeciras to Ceuta and, later, Tangier. With a capacity for 100 cars or 12 railway coaches the two were later joined by a third ship the *Ciudad de Tarifa*.

Although Bland Line for many years operated between Gibraltar and Tangier

The **Biladi** (ex **Liberte**) at the old port of Tangier. (Matthew Murtland)

Acciona Trasmediterranea's **Ciudad de Malaga** at Algeciras, with the **Alcantara Dos** (ex **Tallink Autoexpress**) beyond. (Matthew Murtland)

The Euroferrys **Atlantica** (ex **Stena Jutlandica** of 1973) served Moroccan routes from 1999 until 2010, when she was reportedly sold for scrap having spent a final summer operating between Almeria and Nador. (Matthew Murtland)

*Grandi Navi Veloci's impressive fast cruise ferry **Excelsior** is deployed on the Genoa-Barcelona-Tangier route and is seen arriving at the Italian port. (Matthew Murtland)*

*The **Juan J Sister** helps to maintain the services from Almeria and Malaga to Melilla - this image captures the ship on the berth at the Spanish enclave. Delivered to Trasmed. by Kvaerner-Masa in Turku 12 months after the same yard completed Brittany Ferries' **Normandie**, certain similarities in detail and styling can be seen between the two vessels. (Matthew Murtland)*

*COMANAV's flagship, the **Marrakech** of 1986, is used on the long crossing between the French port of Sete and Tangier, where she is seen at the old ferry port. (Matthew Murtland)*

using the Ailsa, Troon-built car ferry *Mons Calpe* of 1954 (often disrupted by General Franco closing the Gibraltar border), serious competition on services from Spain itself did not come until a Moroccan company, Lignes Maritimes du Detroit (LIMADET), introduced a modern car ferry on a Tangier–Malaga service in 1966 (the Spanish port later becoming Algeciras). LIMADET traced their origins back to the 1863-founded Compagnie de Navigation Paquet but for this new venture were supported by the Norwegian Otto Thoresen. The ship, named *Ibn Batouta* in honour of the Tangier-born scholar and traveller, was given an orange hull in line with Thoresen's English Channel ferries.

Another competitor, Islena de Navegacion (ISNASA) brought their passenger-only *Menorca* into service between Algeciras and Ceuta in 1973. The subsequent history of ISNASA is one of the most fascinating of all ferry operators, involving bull fighting, suicide, murder, repeated financial troubles and adverse newspaper headlines ('floating coffins cross the Straits'). In this context it was perhaps not a tremendous shock or indeed a great loss when the company went bankrupt for a final time in 1998 but in the interim ISNASA provided four distinctive and attractive purpose-built car ferries for use on the services out of Algeciras: the 1980-built *Bahia de Cadiz*, *Bahia de Ceuta*, *Bahia de Malaga* and *Punta Europa*.

COMARIT AND COMANAV

The state-owned Compagnie Marocaine de Navigation (COMANAV) moved into the ferry sector in 1974 when they acquired the German ferry *Prinz Hamlet II* to establish a new, longer-distance route from Tangier to the French port of Sete. Renamed the *Agadir*, the ship was refurbished with decor in an appropriately Moorish style and operated successfully on the 38-hour crossing for 12 years before COMANAV upgraded operations with the introduction of a purpose-built ship. Today that vessel, the stylish *Marrakech*, remains the Moroccan ferry flagship, having almost exclusively served the Tangier–Sete service since being delivered by Chantiers de l'Atlantique in 1986. On board, she further developed the distinctly Moroccan theme but with more of a cruise ferry aspect, with a nightclub, cinema, conference room, lido area and, according to her introductory brochure, clay pigeon shooting.

On the shorter crossings from Algeciras more competition arrived in 1984 from a somewhat unexpected source. The Norwegian Fred. Olsen company had long successfully operated in the Canary Islands but now turned their attention to the Strait of Gibraltar, forming a joint venture, the Compagnie Maritime Maroco-Norvegienne (COMARIT) with Moroccan interests. The former Skagerrak ferry the *Bismillah* (ex *Buenavista*) was introduced on the Tangier–Algeciras route, being joined four years later by the 'Papenburger' *Boughaz* (ex *Viking 5*).

In 1993 LIMADET introduced a remarkable second ship, the *Ibn Batouta 2*, whose distinctive decor, with Moorish arches separating the public rooms and timber screens dividing the saloons into smaller compartments, was designed specifically to accommodate large Moroccan families travelling together. Sadly, the ship's career with LIMADET was short, passing to Trasmediterranea in 1998 and then the Croatian Jadrolinija in 2004, where she remains as their *Zadar*. She was replaced by a further *Ibn Batouta*, the former Sealink *St Christopher*, a ship whose twin freight decks provided many potential practical benefits, but with little of the Moroccan charm of her predecessor.

FERRIMAROC

In 1994, after several years of wrangling with the Spanish authorities keen to protect Trasmediterranea from unwanted competition, a new venture, Ferrimaroc, established a service between Nador and Almeria using the former British Rail ferry *St Edmund*, by then named the *Scirocco*. A subsidiary of British company Cenargo, Ferrimaroc's success at Nador initiated something of a rush to operate at the eastern port. COMANAV, who had previously operated seasonal services from Nador to Sete, also added Almeria sailings, the two routes for several years being in the hands of the former P&O 'Super Vikings' *Pride of Hampshire* and *Pride of Le Havre*, whilst LIMADET opened a service in 1997 using the *Beni Ansar* (formerly the Belgian *Prinses Maria-Esmeralda*).

The final demise of ISNASA in 1998 coincided with the arrival of a new Spanish company on the Algeciras–Tangier route, Euroferrys. Initially using ex-ISNASA tonnage, in 1999 the *Euroferrys Atlantica* (the former *Stena Jutlandica* of 1973) was acquired. Whilst the 'Atlantica' sailed to Tangier, chartered fast craft ran to Ceuta before the delivery of the company's own Austal-built catamaran, the *Euroferrys Pacifica*, in 2001. The year 1999 also saw the arrival of a further operator, the Moroccan IMTC (International Maritime Transport Corporation), who acquired the redundant Nordisk Faergefart ferry *Gelting Syd*, renamed her the *Atlas*, and deployed her initially on a relatively long route from Tangier to Cadiz, settling on Algeciras as the Spanish port in 2000.

THE CURRENT SCENE

For many years most of the ferry companies at both Tangier and Nador operated as part of large pools, co-ordinating schedules and prices and pooling receipts. In 2000, the participants in the Algeciras pool were heavily fined by the authorities – not for any form of collusion as such but rather for their obstruction in failing to admit newcomers IMTC into the pool. The system was finally ruled illegal by the European Union in 2005 with an exemption granted in respect of the very peak period of July and August when the ships run around the clock as part of the Operacion Paso Del Estrecho (literally, 'Operation "Crossing the Straits"'), a government initiative which facilitates the movement of up to two million passengers from the Spanish ports to Morocco.

Perhaps the most notable factor affecting Moroccan ferry traffic in the past decade though has been the remorseless rise of the fast car ferry. For a while fast craft were restricted to services to the Spanish enclaves and the pioneer in this regard was Trasmediterranea's *Albayzin* which began sailing from Algeciras to Ceuta in 1995. Private competition on the Ceuta route followed when the Uruguayan operator Buquebus deployed their InCats *Patricia Olivia* and *Ronda Marina* (ex *Stena Lynx II*) in 1997 and yet another 'foreign' concern came onto the scene in the form of the German Forde Reederei Seetouristik (FRS) in 2000. FRS had strong roots in German coastal shipping but it was its involvement in Nordic Jet Line's Helsinki–Tallinn fast ferry operation which gave a first hint of their future bold expansion. Key to FRS's success was the use of the southernmost Spanish port of Tarifa, from which the crossing to Tangier could be made in just 30 minutes. Suffering from length and draft restrictions 'Tarifa' had previously struggled to establish itself as a ferry port, but those limitations posed no difficulties for the fast ferries. Free to build what soon became more than just a niche, FRS quickly grew into the market leader in the local fast ferry trade, particularly with day trippers, and in 2010 they operated a fleet of five fast ferries on routes from both Tarifa and Algeciras to Ceuta and Tangier.

The success of FRS prompted the established Algeciras operators to come together to deploy Trasmediterranea's fast monohull *Alcantara* on a rival service to Tangier in 2003 and since then fast ferries have become ever more dominant on the Strait of Gibraltar passenger services. In 2010 COMARIT, heretofore a conventional ferry loyalist, purchased the *Highspeed 2* and *Highspeed 3* from Hellenic Seaways, deploying them as the *Bissat* and *Boraq* to Tangier from Tarifa, the increasingly cramped Spanish port having previously been almost exclusively the preserve of FRS.

COMARIT-COMANAV

In 2003 a period of dramatic consolidation amongst the various operators began as COMANAV acquired and later absorbed LIMADET before itself being privatised by the Moroccan government in 2007. The company passed to the French container group CMA CGM who, in turn, relinquished operational control of the ferry part of the business to COMARIT in 2009. Meanwhile, Fred. Olsen's involvement in the latter company had ceased in 2008 when their 50 per cent share was disposed of to their partners, the influential Abdelmoula family, headed by the current mayor of Tangier.

Although still retaining different names and liveries, the COMARIT and COMANAV fleets have effectively been integrated for operational purposes. On the Tangier–Algeciras run, a mix of veterans is deployed: COMARIT's *Banasa* (ex *Mette Mols*) and *Boughaz* alongside COMANAV's ex Sealink pair the *Al Mansour* (ex *Reine Astrid*) and the present *Ibn Batouta*. It is fair to say that the COMARIT ships are somewhat better maintained and the *Banasa* in particular benefited from a very substantial early refit following her acquisition in 1996, with glazed cupolas, Moroccan ceramic panels, an elegant two-tier restaurant and bar area aft and a luxurious VIP suite. The *Boughaz* was refitted somewhat less lavishly in 2001 but still provides a very comfortable means of crossing the Straits. The two COMANAV ships in contrast are a little tired both mechanically and in some of the passenger spaces, with little significant work having been carried out since their UK days.

For several years the third COMARIT ship on the Algeciras route was the *Sara I*, (ex *Djursland II*); chartered from Egypt's El Salam Maritime, she technically operated for COMARIT's Spanish subsidiary Lineas Marítimas Europeas. With the two COMANAV ships integrated into the timetable plus the new high speed venture from Tarifa the *Sara I*, something of a creaking time-warp from her Danish days, was superfluous and headed for the scrap yard in early 2010.

On the longer routes, COMANAV's *Ouzoud*, another ship chartered from El Salam, had become a regular on the long, seasonal Tangier–Genoa run which was inaugurated in 2002. Originally TT Lines' *Peter Pan* of 1974, the *Ouzoud* was a splendid veteran, if somewhat run down, but her career finally came to an end for 2010 and instead COMARIT's *Berkane* was used. One of two large ex SNCM ships purchased in 2002 when COMARIT decisively expanded into the longer-distance routes, the *Berkane* (ex *Napoleon*) was given a major refit in early 2010 which saw the addition of a new mosque, shopping 'street' and Moroccan Tea Room whilst her huge tiered cinema was converted into a nightclub. The second of the SNCM pair, the *Biladi* (ex *Liberte* and also extensively refurbished), is used regularly on the Tangier–Sete route alongside 'the national glory', the *Marrakech*.

At Nador and Almeria the COMARIT group's services for summer 2010 were in the hands of four chartered ships alongside COMANAV's *Mistral Express*. The latter, another ex SNCM ship the *Esterel*, is a somewhat austere vessel with a series of large saloons filled with fixed seating but has been a mainstay of Nador–Almeria services since 1997. Her chartered fleet mates were the unlovely ex-Japanese ferry *Bni Nsar* (previously named the *Marrakech Express*), the *Rostock* (ex *Sally Star*, sub chartered from Scandlines) and the TransEuropa Ferries pair *Oleander* (ex *Pride of Free Enterprise*) and *Eurovoyager* (ex *Prins Albert*). The latter operated the seasonal service from the attractive town of Al Hoceima (60 miles west of Nador) to Almeria, bringing back memories not just of the 2009 charter of her sister the *Primrose* (ex-*Princesse Marie-Christine*) but moreover the nine years of the third of the Belgian trio, the *Prinses Maria-Esmeralda*, spent operating in the area as LIMADET's *Beni Ansar*, latterly in a somewhat precarious mechanical state.

ACCIONA TRASMEDITERRANEA

Trasmediterranea, sold upon privatisation in 2002 to the construction conglomerate Acciona, acquired Ferrimaroc in 2004 and then two-ship Euroferrys in 2006; as with the COMARIT group, again all three names have been retained although the combined fleet is effectively treated as one.

The government contract to supply services to Melilla and Ceuta was

The **Sara I** (ex-**Djursland II**) arrives at Tangier in the colours of Lineas Maritimas Europeas - COMARIT's Spanish subsidiary. The ship was sold for scrap in India in April 2010, taking the name **Winner 10** for her final voyage. (Matthew Murtland)

Sealink's former **Galloway Princess** is now **Le Rif** of IMTC and is seen arriving at Algeciras in September 2010. (Bruce Peter)

renewed in 2006 with the new agreement stating that the ships used should be less than 15 years old. The remaining members of the 'Canguro' class which had been mainstays of the Melilla routings were subsequently retired (the *Ciudad de Salamanca* briefly went on to serve a rival operation from Malaga to Al Hoceima) and two former Canary Islands ships the *Santa Cruz de Tenerife* and the *Juan J Sister* have since been deployed on the routes from Almeria and Malaga. Rather lacking the élan of the 'Canguros' these ferries offer a reliable, if somewhat uninspired, transport service – although many passengers now prefer to use the company's fast ferries.

The Almeria–Nador run during peak season relies exclusively on chartered tonnage with each of Acciona's three subsidiaries chartering one ship each. The mainstay recently has been the *Wisteria*, under a long-term charter from current owners TransEuropa Ferries and which provides a relatively upscale operation compared both to her Ferrimaroc predecessors and to many of her competitors. Chartered to operate alongside the *Wisteria* for the summer of 2010 was Tallink's *Regina Baltica* together with the third ship, the now somewhat run-down *Euroferrys Atlantica*, previously used for 11 years on the Tangier–Algeciras route.

At Algeciras, with the *Euroferrys Atlantica* withdrawn, fast craft dominated Acciona's fleet in 2010, save for the recently refurbished *Ciudad de Malaga* on the Ceuta service; one conventional ship which did appear at Tangier was the *Albayzin*, (ex *Maria Grazia On*), a Visentini-built ro-pax chartered from Moby Lines for a new Tangier–Barcelona route under the Ferrimaroc name.

OTHER OPERATORS

The defunct ISNASA had a sister company called FLEBASA Lines which operated to the Balearic islands off Spain's eastern coast. When FLEBASA, too, succumbed in 1998 a new company, Balearia, was born. Balearia grew rapidly and entered the North Africa trade in 2003 when a joint venture, Nautus al-Maghreb, was formed in collaboration with a Spanish-based Moroccan entrepreneur. Operating initially fast ferries to Tangier, the Buquebus operation to Ceuta was acquired in 2007. Subsequent attempts have been made with conventional tonnage, most notably when the brand new *Passio per Formentera* was operated

through the winter of 2009/10 before transferring to her intended Balearic operations.

IMTC, the smallest remaining independent operator, introduced a second ship, *Le Rif* (ex *Galloway Princess*) alongside the *Atlas* in 2002. IMTC offer a fairly basic service and the two ships are largely unchanged from their previous incarnations; despite a serious vehicle deck fire in 2008, the *Le Rif* remains the better of the pair.

Lastly, a new competitor on the long-distance routes is *Grandi Navi Veloci* (GNV) who from late 2006 extended the Genoa–Barcelona sailings of their fast cruise ferries to Tangier. The ships employed in 2010 were the *Excelsior* and the *Majestic*, certainly the most impressive ferries ever to have sailed regularly to Morocco – although in some areas a little less polished than GNV's core Italian domestic services.

THE FUTURE

Only three of the 35 ferries in use in the summer peak of 2010 were specifically built for operations to North Africa and indeed no purpose-built conventional ferry has entered service since Trasmediterranea's *Ciudad de Malaga* in 1998. There remains a reliance on a seasonal influx of chartered tonnage, although now sourced from perhaps more reputable owners than El Salam. For the North European enthusiast of vintage ferries this makes the area fascinating, with even redundant fast ferry tonnage such as the former *Stena Lynx II* and Hoverspeed's *Diamant* (both now of Balearia) passing for operation in the Strait of Gibraltar.

In the longer term, there remain proposals for a tunnel beneath the Strait, with the most recent, optimistic, estimate that this could be completed by 2025. It is hard to envisage too many of the already antiquated fleet of conventional ferries lasting that long and, with no coherent tonnage investment strategies presently being displayed by any of the main operators, there seems little doubt that for many years to come passengers will be sipping mint tea on the boat decks of old and, occasionally, decrepit tonnage as they make their passage to the North Moroccan coast.

The **Boughaz** was originally the Papenburg-built **Viking 5** of Rederi AB Sally (Viking Line). The penultimate of a remarkable class of nine similar ships she has now operated for COMARIT between Tangier and Algeciras for over twenty years. (Bruce Peter)

COMANAV's **Ibn Batouta** (*ex-***St Christopher***) is seen manoeuvring into dry dock in Gibraltar in September 2010 in advance of a major mechanical overhaul. (Bruce Peter)*

11 Stena Hollandica - The Biggest to Date

by Miles Cowsill

In 2007, Stena Line spent £130 million on lengthening the ro-pax ferries Stena Hollandica and Stena Britannica for the Harwich-Hook of Holland service. They were built in 2001 and 2003 respectively and both were stretched to 240 metre, the same as their successors which entered service in 2010. The lane-metre capacity of the Stena Hollandica rose to 4,000 from 2,500, while that of Stena Britannica jumped to 4,200 from 3,400. In spite of this investment Stena Line took the bold step later in the year to order two giant ferries to replace them at cost of £375 million.

The world's largest ro-pax ferry the *Stena Hollandica* entered commercial service between Harwich and the Hook of Holland on 16th May, heralding her as the biggest ferry in the world. Until her arrival in the North Sea, the Irish Ferries' *Ulysees* had been the world's biggest ferry able to carry some 300 trailers and 134 cars.

When the two German-built ships were ordered in 2007, a very different trading environment prevailed. Not only during the last three years has there been a difficult commercial trading world, with a drop in traffic due to the worldwide downturn, but also whilst the ships were being built at Wismar in Germany the ownership of the yard changed four times during their construction period. The new ships were ordered to stem the demise of passengers and cars on the route, offering better passenger facilities, in the light of the earlier errors that led to the withdrawl of the conventional services of the *Koningin Beatrix* and *Stena Europe*, in favour of the HSS operation.

Unlike most modern day ro-pax ferries, Stena Ro-Ro who financed and oversaw the construction, admit that both new ships are more like a passenger ship put on top of a four-deck freight vessel, compared to most ro-pax ferries where the superstructure stretches only half the ships's

Until the delivery of the **Stena Hollandica** Irish Ferries' **Ulysses** held the accolade of being the largest ferry in the world. The **Ulysses** is seen here arriving at Holyhead in February 2010 from Dublin. (Miles Cowsill)

length. Whilst both vessels are now the largest of their type in the world, cosiderable efforts were made to optimise the hull form in tank tests. Stena Ro-Ro are very pleased with the design of the hull form and surprisingly it is better than expected with vibration levels being reduced to a minimum with both ships achieving a 'Comfort 2' classification. A lot of this success has been achieved by incorporating in the stern a lip, while the bow features a long surface-piercing bulbous bow.

The *Stena Hollandica* was the first of the pair of identical ships to go for sea trials on 26th March. Prior to her delivery she carried out extensive trials in the Baltic and berthing trials. The 'Hollandica' was officially named by Princess Margrit of the Netherlands on 8th June. The *Stena Hollandica* under the Dutch flag was joined in October 2010 by her sister-ship the *Stena Britannica* which flies the Red Ensign, continuing the tradition of the route of the two nations. With the delivery of the *Stena Britannica* sees the completion of the largest-ever new tonnage investment by Stena Line. Both ships will probably hold the title as the world's largest ferries for many years in the current world economic climate.

On entry into service in May, the *Stena Hollandica* took over from the older and smaller *Stena Hollandica* on the daily roster of the 14.30 sailing from Holland, with a return from Harwich at 23.45 the same day. The the *Stena Britannica*, on entry into service, of was rostered to operate from Parkeston Quay at 09.00 with a return sailing to Holland at 22.00.

Pim de Lang, Managing Director of Stena Line BV, quite openly admits that there has been a drop in demand in freight since the new ships were ordered but he is confident that the route is in an ideal position to capitalise when Europe comes out of recession.

Both the 'Hollandica' and 'Britannica' have the equivalent of 5.5 kilometres of vehicle space. The German twins have twin-level loading at both the bow and stern and three main vehicle decks, plus a lower hold

In 2007 Stena Line jumboised both the **Stena Hollandica** and **Stena Britannica**. This view shows the 'Hollandica' having this work undertaken at the German yard of Lloyd Werft. (Stena Line)

*An impressive view of the **Stena Hollandica** undergoing sea trials off the German coast. (Stena Line)*

able to take 310 freight vehicles or trailers, whilst mezzanine decks on the port side of Deck 3 level can take some 230 cars.

Currently the route carries some 450,000 passengers a year and with both ships having a capacity for 1,200 with a total of 1,376 beds available in 538 cabins on Decks 10 and 11, there is more than adequate capacity to expand passenger levels with these giant ferries. The standard cabins offer capacity for five people, with one of the single berths being a double bed and the other three berths being for single occupancy. All cabins feature wider beds than found on other ferries and have a specially designed deep mattress for extra comfort. The vessels also offer a range of deluxe cabins where there has always been a good demand with business travel.

Figura Arkitekter were responsible for the interior design of the new ships. They started work on the project in 2007, the year after the orders had been placed. In talks with the yard and the owner, Figura established the general layout, elevations of bulkheads, colour schemes, and so forth. As the ships will operate on a 6½-hour service that includes both morning and evening sailings, the requirements for the interiors were greater than for a ferry operating on a shorter crossing.

Figura responded to this challenge by introducing the Living Room concept, an area where passengers can read books and magazines, watch a wide-screen TV and where Bluetooth service is available, all free of charge.

The design on Stena Line's vessels follows a similar service concept throughout the fleet. It is based on Scandinavian modern design, with lots of light wood used in the interiors. Figura has worked with Stena Line since 1986 and have built up a good relationship with the company during that period. During the almost quarter century of cooperation

The **Stena Hollandica** emerges from her builder's undercover shed in which most of her construction was undetaken. (Stena Line)

that Stena Line and Figura have behind them, the ferry company has created a visual image that embraces not just the ships and their interiors, but also terminals and offices.

A well-structured service concept has emerged from this relationship, however, this does not mean that every ship in the fleet offers exactly the same amenities; what is available depends on the service that a vessel in question operates on and its age.

The main passenger area can be found on Deck 9 with the forward section offering superb views. In this part of both ships there is a self-service restaurant, branded as the Taste Restaurant and the la carte

The **Stena Britannica** was delivered to Stena Line in October 2010. She is seen here leaving Harwich during her first couple of days in service on the UK/Dutch route. (Ian Boyle)

The **Stena Hollandica** arrives at the Hook of Holland for the first time from Germany. The completely new infrastructure had to be designed at both the Dutch and UK ports to accommodate these giant vessels. (Henk van der Lugt)

Both the **Stena Hollandica** and **Stena Britannica** have an impressive array of car decks over four levels and can accommodate up to 5,666 metres of lane capacity. This view shows Deck 5. (Stena Line)

Metropolitan Restaurant on the starboard side. Included in this area is the Riva Bar, designed in the style of Italian speed boats, a wine bar, a casino, children's play-room and smokers' lounge. Stena Line have moved away from the 'Food City' experience with these new ships, which has allowed them to be more flexible with their operations at different times of the day. To the aft of both ships there is a luxuriously fitted-out Stena Plus Lounge, the Barista Bar and lounge areas, plus an internet room, cinema, conference room and separate truckers' restaurant bar and lounge, especially designed to cater for the needs of freight drivers. In the central section of Deck 9 there is a starboard shopping area, information desk and bureau de change. The café, bureau de change facility and reception is open throughout all crossings. A small sun deck bar and outside seating are also available on two deck areas on Decks 9 and 10 of the German-built ships. The lorry drivers have their own areas on both ships where they are able drink, eat and watch TV - the truckers are so valued that they are even allowed to cook their own meal!

Both ferries have four MAN engines consisting of two 9,600 kW and two 7,200 kW units which are able to offer quicker crossings than that of the previous vessels on the route by some half an hour. The German-built ships are designed to have as low an environmental impact as possible. Obviously each ship has catalytic converters, improved hull design, highly efficient engines and the best possible fuel combustion but they also have facilities to recycle glass, cardboard and food waste aboard and solar film treatments to windows will exclude up to 82 per cent of the sun's radiant heat, reducing the energy used by the on-board air-conditioning systems.

The previous *Stena Britannica* and *Stena Hollandica*, which have offered valiant service on the route, were sent to Germany for extension of their

One of the Captain's Class cabins offered on both vessels, with a large double bed, a mini-bar, TV and large shower room. Stena Line market these cabins as rooms as a hotel would on land. (Stena Line)

accommodation prior to being renamed and transferred to the lucrative Gothenburg-Kiel service. The transfer of these two ships to the Gothenburg-Kiel service will increase freight capacity on that route by 30%.

The introduction of the world's biggest car ferries on the Harwich-Hook of Holland service will ultimately see a change of approach with other operators and possibly the demise of other tonnage on the North Sea over the next couple of years.

*The Metropolitan Restaurant pictured on the starboard side of the **Stena Hollandica**. (Stena Line)*

The Stena Plus Lounge on board **Stena Hollandica** and her sister has been specifically designed for comfort and quietness from other passengers and includes a business centre. (Stena Line)

This view shows the extensive eating area forward on both the 'Britannica' and 'Hollandica', which includes the Taste Restaurant, Riva Bar, Taste Wine Bar and Casino. (Stena Line)

12 Photo Feature - Piraeus
by John May

Over the last 20 years the ships making their way out of the harbours at Piraeus have seen enormous change. In the early 1990s it was normal to find a dozen car ferries making early morning departures for the island ports of the Aegean and for almost all to have spent their early careers in Scandinavian or British waters, with a few more exotic creations from local shipyards based on ships that had been built for service in Japan. Cruise ships were mainly Greek flagged and on short itineraries around the ancient sites of the Eastern Mediterranean with occasional visits by former liners then in cruise service such as P&O's iconic *Canberra*.

A generation on and the economy of Greece has blossomed through the brief but painfully expensive phase of hosting the Olympic Games, has passed its zenith and now faces a period of severe austerity. The ships have changed in many ways. The previous generation of ferries have almost all departed for demolition on Indian and Turkish beaches, to be replaced partly by newly built vessels from the shipyards of Italy and the Far East but also by a proliferation of fast craft. The current generation of large cruise ships have seen off many of the smaller ships and sail on less culturally based itineraries.

Yet the port of Piraeus continues to fascinate, perhaps nowhere else can such a variety of passenger shipping be seen and experienced close up in 2011. Despite the unfriendly application of some of the tedious restrictions of the ISPS security regime that apparently makes American tourists feel safe at the cost of much inconvenience to the real traveller while separating the population from the ships that are part of their community, it is still possible to experience the vibrancy of one of the main ports of Europe in hot and stimulating conditions as these photos demonstrate.

One of the most remarkable features of Piraeus is the large sheltered bay just outside the port separating the mainland from the urbanised island of Salamis. Around the shores are a mass of yards that specialise in the conversion and maintenance of the ships serving Greek ports. Until the middle of the last decade this was populated by many ships that had long since reached the end of their working lives but were kept by their owners against the day that demand for ships or scrap metal increased. A rapid rise in steel prices and a growing realisation that ships built in the 1960s and not subject to much modernisation would not be suitable for service in the 21st century has seen many depart for recycling into consumer goods but a few remain. Even in high summer these chains of long laid-up vessels were to be found off the Perama shore.

Among various freighters can be seen (fourth from left) the **Oceanis** *which was built in 1962 as Townsend Car Ferries'* **Free Enterprise I**, *converted for day cruising but which has not seen service since 2007. Sixth from left is the* **Panagia Krimniotissa** *which had been built in 1973 and spent the first 15 years of her life in Japan before conversion to a freight Ro-Ro latterly used by SAOS Ferries which ceased most of its operations in 2008. The right hand group has on either side the* **Duchess M** *(previously the* **Breizh Izel** *in the Brittany Ferries fleet) which last operated for Marlines in 2008 and on the right another ex-Japanese ferry the* **European Express**, *which has seen service in various parts of the Mediterranean since coming to Europe in 1999 and has since been taken on charter in the later part of the summer of 2010 by NEL Lines.*

Typical of the vessels now using the port are Celebrity Cruises **Celebrity Summit** *of 2001 baking under the July sun as Blue Star Ferries'* **Blue Star Naxos**, *built in 2002 in Korea arrives. In the distance cargo vessels turn gently on their anchor chains off the island of Aegina.*

The neat lines of Hellenic Seaways' **Nefeli** *partially disguise her origins as the* **Mukogawa**, *a trim 3,750 ton ferry built in 1990 for service in the Japanese islands but which has now spent more than half her life on her current owners' shorter distance routes.*

Under their previous manifestation as Minoan Flying Dolphins, Hellenic Seaways replaced a large fleet of ex-Sealink ferries in the early years of the present century with newly built catamarans including the **Highspeed 4**, built in Australia by Austal. While the opportunity of long voyages on deck is denied to her passengers, the 40 knot speed of the vessel allows her to fit in double the frequency of sailings given by her predecessors and she is accordingly far more productive for her owners.

Typical of the first generation of fast craft in Greek waters which accustomed many Greek travellers to the idea of a sea voyage being quick, noisy and uncomfortable - the **Hermes** of Aegean Flying Dolphins passes out of Piraeus en route for Aegina. She is a Russian-built Kometa class hydrofoil built in 1981 but re-engined in the late 1990s. Behind her and with her stern dissolving in the exhaust from the older craft's engines is the former Superseacat Three which now sails as **Speedrunner III**.

Seen departing from the Great Harbour of Piraeus on a sailing to Santorini, the **Blue Star Naxos** *offers an on-board experience not unlike that which her builders at Daewoo provide in their inexpensive and unremarkable cars.*

The more familiar outline of the Van der Giessen built **Blue Star 1** *occupies a quay beside the modern port control building while loading for a sailing to Rhodes. She has returned to the Aegean after spending 2007 and 2008 on the company's now abandoned route linking Rosyth with Zeebrugge. In the foreground a modern version of the traditional caique passes out of the harbour bound for Salamis.*

Older cruise ships still work out of Piraeus on short itineraries and here Louis Cruises' **The Aegean Pearl** is seen at the beginning of a three-day circuit. Built for Kloster in 1971 as the **Southward**, she has recently been sold on to Israeli interests to continue trading to continue in a career now in its fortieth year.

Early mornings still provide a rush of departures around 08.00 and here Hellenic Seaways' **Nefeli** on a sailing to Aegina is passed by her owner's **Highspeed 3** en route to the islands of the Western Cyclades (prior to her recent sale to Morocco) while closer by the **Super Jet**, a passenger catamaran which has sailed in the Aegean since delivery in 1995.

Among the last of the classic car ferries of the 1970s to remain in service, the **Hengist** was built in 1972 to operate for Sealink from Folkestone and came to Greece in 1992. She now sails for Ventouris Sea Lines on a year-round itinerary to Milos and the Western Cyclades with a regular early morning departure from Piraeus.

Some of the older vessels have seen little service since 2008 and many have been laid up in the Great Harbour awaiting sale, which it has become increasingly clear will not be for further service. Here four examples are moored to the north of the harbour entrance - the bulk of the **Anthi Marina** (originally Townsend Thoresen's **Spirit of Free Enterprise** of 1980) lies behind the same owner's **Milena** (originally built in Japan in 1970) and the Italian-built **Dimitroula** of 1978. Nearer the camera the Ro-Ro **Panagia Agiasou** of SAOS Ferries was also built in Japan in 1973 and began her lay-up in 2009.

A brief joint operation between Greek and Italian owners styled as Kallisti Ferries came to a messy conclusion wrapped in the tentacles of Greek bureaucracy. After the collapse of the operation the **Sardinia Vera** was seen laid up and awaiting a tow back to Italy. She had spent her early career on charter in Canada and sailed out of Newhaven for five years at the start of the century.

Possibly destined to be the last survivor of her generation, the well-maintained **Vitsentzos Kornaros** of Lane Lines of Eastern Crete was originally Townsend Thoresen's Viking Viscount of 1976 before a long spell in P&O colours as the **Pride of Winchester**.

Current operations are typified by this afternoon scene of Hellenic Seaways **Nissos Chios** loading as the **Blue Star Naxos** makes another of her frequent arrivals. The design of the smaller ship is clearly reflected in her half sister, also ordered by Blue Star but from a Greek yard and heavily delayed before being rejected by them, she was eventually completed for the rival company to a much higher specification.

The most impressive of the current ferry operators at Piraeus is Minoan Lines who, in addition to routes in the Adriatic, operate the **Festos Palace** of 2001 on a daily service to Heraklion in Crete.

New Titles from Ferry Publications

Two New Ships, One New Era

In 2011 P&O Ferries will introduce the Spirit of Britain and Spirit of France as the new generation of cross-channel ferries. The background and development and construction of the largest ferries ever built for the Dover-Calais service are brought together in this new book, published in January 2011. Wealth of photography of the construction of both ships and interviews. 128 pages. Price £22.00.

Queen Elizabeth

This book from Philip Dawson continues our series of the current Cunard fleet. The book covers the development and construction of Cunard's new cruise ship Queen Elizabeth with outstanding views of her construction and delivery. Price £18.50.

DFDS – Sailing in Style

This book draws on the archive material from DFDS and maritime libraries in Denmark to bring the reader a wealth of outstanding pictures of this historic company. A narrative text gives an insight to support the book with easy and readable captions. Price £21.50.

All at Sea

This quality title includes many of the outstanding views painted by marine artist Robert Lloyd. Robert Lloyd's paintings over the last 25 years range from historical views of Cunard and P&O ships, plus a variety of cargo, coasters, ferries and tankers. This quality book brings together many of his outstanding illustrations with background on the views and ships from the respective companies illustrated. 128 pages. Price £22.00.

Solent Seaways

This new and expanded version of the history of Wightlink's services to the Isle of Wight is compiled by John Hendy and looks at the history of the Portsmouth-Fishbourne and the Lymington-Yarmouth routes, together with the introduction of new tonnage on the Lymington service and the new fast ferries between Portsmouth and Ryde. 96 pages. Price £18.50.

The Ferry

This academic work written by Bruce Peter and Philip Dawson covers the history and development of the ferry from the Victorian era to this century. This academic book is supported by a wealth of photography and illustrations. 230 pages. Limited print-run. Price £36.

Passage to the Northern Isles: Ferry Services to Orkney & Shetland

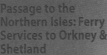

This new edition covering the ferry services to Orkney and Shetland includes recent updates by Miles Cowsill and Colin Smith. The book covers the fascinating history between mainland Scotland and the Northern Isles and includes the development and history of NorthLink's involvement with the operations since 2002. 96 pages. Price £18.50.

Harwich-Hook of Holland

This new historical account traces the route from its origins to the introduction of the world's largest ferries, the Stena Britannica and Stena Hollandica. Full fleet list. Background on construction of new vessels for the route in 2010. Hardback. 128 pages. Price £21.50.

The Ferry – A Drive Through History

This abbreviated publication draws on the academic work of its larger sister publication. This book offers an easy read with outstanding views of ferries over the last 150 years, many of which are different from that of the larger publication. 144 pages. Price £24.50.

Ferries 2011

This new edition of Nick Widdows' annual title features Viking Line, P&O Ferries' new ships for the Dover Calais route and overview of the fast ferry industry. Includes detailed information on all the principal ferry operations of Northern Europe. Full colour. 224 pages. Price £21.30.

Ferries of Belgium

This new book compiled by Mike Louagie with his outstanding library of photographs around the Belgian ports. The book includes many of the ferries that have served Ostend and Zeebrugge over the last 30 years and is supported by easy-to-read and informative captions. Price £18.50.

Cruise Ships of Dover

Photographer John Mavin brings together outstanding views of many cruise ships which have visited Dover in the last ten years and looks at the development of Dover as a cruise ship port. Many photographs with easy-to-read captions plus map of the port. Price 18.00.

FERRY Publications

Order online from
www.ferrypubs.co.uk
By telephone on
+44 (0)1624 898446
By post from
PO Box 33, Ramsey, Isle of Man, IM99 4LP
All prices shown above include UK P&P.
Overseas orders please add a further £1.85 per order.